Praise for Am I the One?

"Jim Lucas manages to shoot from the hip, hit the nail on the head, and score a slam dunk . . . all without breaking a sweat. His approach is dead on. I may run out of clichés, but I haven't run out of good things to say about *Am I the One?*"

> Bob Hostetler, coauthor with Josh McDowell
> *Don't Check Your Brains at the Door, Why True Love Waits,*
> *The Love Killer,* and *Beyond Belief to Convictions*

"*Am I the One?* is a fantastic book, and one that I see the need for very often. I know it will be a great blessing as it gets into the hands of Christian young people across the country."

> Dr. Joe White, President, Kanakuk Kamp
> Promise Keepers speaker, and Author of
> *Parents Guide to Spiritual Mentoring of Teens,*
> *What Kids Wish Parents Knew about Parenting,*
> and *Pure Excitement*

"If you're on a quest for finding the right marriage partner, don't take another step without this valuable book. *Am I the One?* is biblically based and filled with dozens of practical pointers for finding 'the one.'"

> Drs. Les and Leslie Parrott, Seattle Pacific University
> Authors of *Saving Your Marriage Before It Starts*

"*Am I the One?* is, for youth and young adults, the best book on relationships that I have ever read. . . . James Lucas avoids all of the typical pitfalls that so many dating book authors fall into. He doesn't give you a list of don'ts—don't date (the trendy rule), don't kiss, don't do this, don't do that, and everything will be OK. Because, as I think we all know deep down, the outward rules are meaningless if the inside isn't in the proper order. . . . Lucas sets solid principles . . . that help you ask the right questions of yourself. . . . *Am I the One?* is a must-read."

> Michael S. Janke, Columnist, *CMCentral.com*

"I love it! . . . This book is the sweet spot! I love how James Lucas presents the case in an honest, straightforward way. . . . I also like how the book is written for a diverse audience. Mr. Lucas caters to every single type of teenager there is. In this book, there is something for everyone. . . . In short, this is one book that is able to transcend all genders and races and nationalities and get to the heart of the matter—showing teens how to see their qualities and their flaws and know how to love themselves in spite of [the flaws], which is how God loves us. . . . This book is going to become the 'sweet spot' for many people."

Sarah Brown, Cast Member
"TruthQuest: California" Reality TV

"TruthQuest [books are] a great way to strengthen a daily walk with Christ."

The Guys of Plus One
(Music Artists)

"Because Lucas believes finding the 'right one' starts with being the 'right one,' he encourages readers to reflect on who they're becoming. Then he explores various search aspects—using Scripture, real-life examples, discussion questions, and checklists (including '12 Lousy Reasons for Getting Married'). . . .

"[Am I the One?] is a fascinating read. The book raises some excellent points, and its serious approach to marriage will make young readers think twice before jumping into relationships . . . the message applies to all singles."

Christy Simon, *CBA Marketplace*
"Book Reviews"

TruthQuest™

am i the one?

CLUES TO *FINDING & BECOMING*
A PERSON WORTH MARRYING

JAMES R. LUCAS
STEVE KEELS, general editor

BROADMAN
& HOLMAN
PUBLISHERS

NASHVILLE, TENNESSEE

© 2002 by James Lucas
All rights reserved
Printed in the United States of America

0-8054-2573-X

Published by Broadman & Holman Publishers,
Nashville, Tennessee

Dewey Decimal Classification: 158
Subject Heading: SELF-IMPROVEMENT \ DATING (SOCIAL CUSTOMS)

Unless otherwise noted, Scripture quotations have been taken from the
Holman Christian Standard Bible, © 2000 by Holman Bible Publishers.
Other versions cited are NIV, the Holy Bible, New International Version,
© 1973, 1978, 1984 by International Bible Society; and NLT, the Holy
Bible, New Living Translation, © 1996, used by permission of Tyndale
House Publishers, Inc., Wheaton, Illinois 60189, all rights reserved.

3 4 5 6 7 8 9 10 07 06 05 04

To
Beth

Other Books by James R. Lucas

Family and Other Relationships

The Paradox Principle of Parenting
1001 Ways to Connect with Your Kids
Proactive Parenting: The Only Approach That Really Works
The Parenting of Champions

Fiction

A Perfect Persecution
Noah: Voyage to a New Earth
Weeping in Ramah

Personal Life and Growth

Knowing the Unknowable God:
    How Faith Thrives on Divine Mystery
Walking through the Fire:
    Finding the Purpose of Pain in the Christian Life

Leadership and Organizational Development

The Passionate Organization:
    Igniting the Fire of Employee Commitment
Balance of Power:
    Fueling Employee Power Without Relinquishing Your Own
Fatal Illusions:
    Shredding a Dozen Unrealities That Can Keep Your
    Organization from Success

Visit the Relationship Development Center online at
www.relationshipdevelopmentonline.com

contents

foreword

The first time I met him, I was convinced he was the One. We shook hands and felt electric tingles from our toes all the way to our ring fingers. I would call up my friends, beaming that he was everything I ever dreamed of. His love for God, his charm, his eyes . . . he was perfect! Even three years into our whirlwind relationship, I was more convinced he was my Prince Charming than ever before. I saw him as my personalized IV to all things wonderful. He was the missing link to my ultimate, true identity. This was the One.

When I held his hand, I thought I had held my future. We wrapped ourselves so tightly around the relationship that it rivaled the fiercest Kung-Fu grip! But how was I to know that within the grip of "us" there was a hand extended to the seemingly *impossible* . . . that we were *not* the Ones for one another?

Perhaps you have gone through the same thing at one time or another. Could that be why you've reached for this book? Maybe you were like me—in love with love. Maybe you are just beginning to step into a new season of emotions with a possible prospect in view. You could be on this quest on your own. In any case, you are in luck. You have found the right book. If you've ever desired to be wanted, wise, and one day wed, keep reading. Inside, you will discover the how tos and the how nots to finding the One. Turn the pages further, and you will be challenged to reach a deeper place of loving God so that you can love someone else like never before.

~ *Joy Williams*
recording artist

acknowledgments

Big-time thanks go to Gary Terashita, my can't-be-beat editor at Broadman & Holman. He had a strong vision for this project from the very first. This is my second book with Gary, and I hope we get to do many more together. Gary, you're a great friend, a sharp thinker, a great blend of seriousness and humor, and a man with a genuine heart for God, people, and excellence. Also, it's fabulous—and scary—to find someone who reminds me so much of me.

I very much appreciate the support and encouragement of Steve Keels, the general editor for the TruthQuest series. Steve has so much experience with young people that I was concerned how well he would like the material. Steve, you'll never know how much your comment, "This material hits the sweet spot," hit my sweet spot. Thanks for putting this great series together for young people who want to live a life that counts.

The rest of the team at Broadman & Holman has, as always, done a stellar job on this project. Lisa Parnell, the project editor, has superbly shepherded this through the maze that producing a book always is. Lisa, you've kept everything—including me—moving along at a nice clip. I also want to thank George Knight, who worked hard to make this material accessible to everyone who reads this book. Thanks to each and every one of you.

When it came time to make sure that the book is, in every detail, relevant, accurate, excellent, and worthy of a reader's time, I turned the manuscript over to Laura Lucas. She read through every word and every line, and made an incredible number of improvements to the work. She brought her many years of teaching and working with young people, and her extensive education and knowledge, fully into play. Laura, this is a substantially better

book because of your involvement and care—you improve everything you touch. I also want to thank her colleague and friend
(and my friend), Jenn Prentice, for taking time out of a packed
schedule to bring her great insights and suggestions to the work.
Jenn, you're dynamite! David and Beth Lucas, dynamic people in
their own right, made sure I remembered that the book was written for people their age, and made many good comments on the
book. I hope you both get to live the best of what this book is all
about. I have gotten to watch four young people up close and personal—Laura, Peter, David, and Beth. Thanks for letting me be part
of your lives.

Members of my staff at the Relationship Development Center
have also worked hard to make this project a reality. Maryl Janson
gave ongoing encouragement, bounced these ideas off young
people in a variety of settings, and gave many suggestions for
improving the material. Maryl, your enthusiasm is inspiring. And,
as always, Priscilla Buchanan has worked to keep everything in our
office—including me—positive, joyful, and focused on having an
impact. Priscilla, your care is priceless.

My family has been, in all ways, exceptionally supportive. You
are The One.

Finally, my thanks to T. O. for your inspiration and encouragement.

introduction

In the movie *The Matrix*, a hard-pressed underground of humans is fighting for freedom from man-made machines. They need someone special to lead them.

They risk everything to find that person. Morpheus, the driving force behind the underground movement, finally finds him in the unlikely person named Thomas Anderson, a low-level computer programmer whose online alias is Neo. Morpheus tells his other people that he has found their leader. He tells them he has found *the one.*

But there are tests—physical, mental, emotional, and philosophical—that Neo has to pass before everyone (including Neo) can really *know* he is the one. One of the signs is in the form of a prophecy given to the story's heroine, Trinity. At the end of the movie, we all know that Neo is the one, for both the movement and for Trinity. But it has taken a lot of gut-checking for everyone to really know. Neo's gut-checking started with having to make a choice between a blue pill and a red pill. Gut-checks *always* start with a choice.

That's what this book is about—not a blue pill or a red pill but a choice much more critical than that. You need to be thinking straight and acting right when you decide on whether you want to spend the rest of your life with someone.

You may still be a long way from making this decision. But it's never too early to begin thinking about some important matters that can prepare you for this crucial phase of your life.

So settle back and open your mind. It's my job to make you think—but I'll try to be gentle! I hope you enjoy the ride on your way to finding *the one.*

Building a Solid Foundation for Relationships

Part 1

It's wonderful to be young! Enjoy every minute of it.
Do everything you want to do; take it all in.
Ecclesiastes 11:9 NLT

"all i wanna do is have some fun"

chapter 1

You're young!

Very cool.

You're young, and you want to have a good time. You don't mind being serious when you need to be, but you really just want to enjoy your life. You've got a chance to be and do in a way that will never be quite the same, never be *yours*, again.

And you like the sound of the opening Bible verse above. Never heard *that* one before! It *is* wonderful to be young! Unlike a lot of "church people," God is telling you that it is perfectly all right to "enjoy every minute of it."

And more: He tells you to "do everything you want to do." Wow! You don't even know what that "everything" is or means—it's hard to take it all in—but it sure does sound terrific.

In other words, it's OK with God that you want to have fun.

Don't let the excitement of youth cause you to forget your Creator.
Ecclesiastes 12:1 NLT

Fun

The first thing we'd better do is say again that God isn't against fun. In fact, He *created* fun. The only reason that there is anything at all on this earth to enjoy is that God put it here. And He put a *lot* of it here.

So if religion and church aren't fun, it's not God's fault. If true fun gets spoiled, people rather than God are doing the spoiling. Why? Because most people don't know how to have fun, including most "church" people. Many of them are skilled at hating fun and judging fun and stopping fun. Don't blame God for the unpleasant, unfun things that people who claim to be Christians do. God is the one who turns our "wailing into dancing" (Psalm 30:11 NIV).

So what is "fun"?

The dictionary defines "fun" as "something that provides mirth or amusement." Wow, that is really boring! Not to mention shallow.

So what kinds of things are fun? Well, movies are fun. Music is fun. Good food and fellowship are very fun. Scary rides and scary sports can be great fun. Driving a car and being able to go where you want is fun. Getting to make your own choices is scary at times, but it is also a boatload of fun. Having someone compliment you is so much fun that Mark Twain said, "I can live for three months on a good compliment."

But more fun than any of that is to be with the right kind of people. There are people who will make your heart sing. There are people who will bring you closer to God. There are people who will make you laugh and there are people who will make you cry—the good kind of cry, the cry that says you're finding out who you are and what life is all about.

You want a significant relationship? Now *that's* fun. It is really fun to be with someone who likes you, who thinks you're something special, who makes you feel like no one else makes you feel. And God is totally for this kind of relationship. God said, "It is not good for the man to be alone" (Genesis 2:18 NIV), and this is *when*

God Himself was hanging out with him, "walking in the garden in the cool of the day" (Genesis 3:8b NIV). In life, it can't be just "me and God." God said that wasn't enough. God Himself said that "it is not good" for a human being to be without close relationships with other human beings.

We all want at least one or two of these special relationships. Just don't assume that a relationship with someone of the opposite sex or that marriage will automatically provide it. Marriage doesn't automatically provide *anything,* except for "various trials" (James 1:2).[1]

So what kinds of things *aren't* fun? Well, movies and music that leave you feeling empty or dirty aren't fun. Drinking can seem fun at the time, but the results can be very unfun. Getting a ticket, wrecking a car, or hitting a pedestrian are not fun. Making choices while stubbornly ignoring all advice is guaranteed to lead to anywhere but fun. Having someone put you down or make fun of you is, ironically, no fun at all.

But less fun than any of that is to be with the wrong kind of people. There are people who will make your heart weep. There are people who will pull you away from God. There are people who will make you laugh at others and cry when you don't get everything your way (or theirs).

There are people who will offer you a significant relationship but not really mean it. Now *that's* not fun. They might not even intend to harm you, but they are so broken or confused that they don't know how to love you, don't know how to care about you, don't know how to do anything but hurt and wound and tear you down. And there are people who really *will* intend to harm you. They won't advertise it—in fact, if they're really good at destruction, they'll put on an act that could win an Oscar.

We don't want any of these relationships, but that's what many people will offer you. That's what the Enemy will offer you. A lot of people don't see these people for what they are until they marry them, which is way too late to do them any good.

We need to talk about one more category: Things that ought to be fun but usually aren't. Like a lot of the time we spend at school. Most homework. Many discussions with parents and older people in general. The great majority of jobs. And a big percentage of stuff that goes on at church, which should be a road to fun and joy and depth of purpose but is way too often a road to judgment city and boredom. Teachers and parents and bosses and pastors have a lot of explaining to do for the fun they have missed or destroyed.

The least boring person in existence is God. He knows how to have a good time. He *knows* how, which means we have to *learn* how. So here's the biggest news: The only way to really have fun, and to *continue* to have fun, is to do it God's way. You can't even *start* to have real fun unless you've got God in the middle of it all. Anything else is just illusion.

The Price

Erin had never seen anyone as cool as Brendan. He didn't say much at the Bible studies, but when he did—wow, he sounded so smart! And wise. And sure of himself. He was always doing interesting things, and everyone seemed to listen up when he described them. And he was really hot. Best of all, he *only* wanted to spend time with *her.* He was the most talkative and open guy she had ever known. His cockiness and focus on his own activities bothered her some, and he seemed a little condescending and judgmental when talking about some of their friends. But overall she couldn't imagine a better guy.

Erin might have a chance, right now, right at this moment of possibilities, to mess up the rest of her life. A tremendous chance. In fact, she could be a heartbeat away from making the biggest mistake of her life.

Every day she is getting more and more involved with Brendan. What if his cockiness is really arrogance and a sense of superiority—even toward her? What if his self-focus will one day mean he isn't interested in the details of her life at all? What if his condescension turns into full-blown nastiness, and his judgmental orientation gets turned in *her* direction?

Then, after they're totally involved or engaged or married—this will be a very lousy time to get the answers to those "what ifs."

The price of having fun, of enjoying your life, of continuing to receive the best life has to offer is *vigilance.* Paying attention. Making good choices. Picking up the clues that all is not well. Not being a fool who rushes in where angels fear to tread.

You have the right to have fun and to enjoy your life. Because of that, you also have the right to be miserable and to wreck your life.

The price is high. But you get what you pay for.

The Dream

What an exciting time of life you are in right now!

When we watch a movie that has a good love story, we can almost always see who the "bad guy" is—the person the heroine should avoid like acne. For the *Princess Bride* it was Prince Humperdink, who intended to kill her after their marriage and then frame the kingdom of Gilder for it. In *Ever After,* Danielle sees Pierre le Pieu for what he is and ends up with good Prince Henry. In *The Princess Diaries,* Mia has to see past not-so-great Josh to find the amazing Michael.

Even in real life, some of these bad choices are still obvious. But it's important to remember that things are not always what they appear to be. How will you know what's real, what's a lie, and what's just confused?

The only way is to get past the "dream" view of other people. Nobody is really a dream. Everybody has pimples and warts and flaws. The prettiest girls can be the creepiest. The "hotties" can turn out to be slimy. The "coolest" people can be the most insecure, the most jealous, the most demanding, and the nastiest if they don't get everything their way.

9

Beautiful girls who are a little wild can seem very exciting—they *are* very exciting. But God's assessment? "A beautiful woman who" rejects good sense is "like a gold ring in a pig's snout" (Proverbs 11:22 NIV). You see the gold. But look a little farther. You go *that* way, and you'll be rooting around in the pen with the pigs.

Guys who are good-looking and self-confident and look like they know what they want can seem like a dream. They might *be* a dream—by becoming your nightmare.

One of the hardest lessons for people to learn—most people in their seventies still haven't figured it out—is that other people can put on a good front. They can be great actors who cover up their nastiness and selfishness with a mask. The worst people can appear to be the best people—for awhile. And the very worst is when they pretend to be serious Christians, "disguising themselves as apostles of Christ" (2 Corinthians 11:13). God tells us we shouldn't be surprised: "And no wonder! For Satan himself is disguised as an angel of light. So it is no great thing if his servants also disguise themselves as servants of righteousness" (2 Corinthians 11:14–15).

But the truth is that most people *are* surprised. Paul admonished the Corinthians, "Look at what is obvious" (2 Corinthians 10:7). He told the Galatians that "God does not judge by external appearance" (Galatians 2:6 NIV)—although people do all the time. If you end up being surprised, it's probably because you were only looking on the surface and judging people by appearance. If Erin marries Brendan, she may be in for a surprise, but only if she hasn't been paying attention to the clues.

The lesson is *not* to avoid trusting anyone. The lesson is to be careful whom you trust. The only way to learn is by relating to a lot of people of both sexes—spending time, talking about life, probing values, understanding souls. But the lesson of the Bible and life is that you always—always—need to have your guard up. The person you might be able to trust the most might have just slipped into sin and he doesn't know how to hide it, while the person you should trust the least may hide every sickness in her soul and present herself to you and others as "the super Christian."

How will you know people like this? They are hard to unmask, but here are a few clues:

- They may talk about "higher standards" a lot, but the standards will be made up by them rather than God. (God has written a special warning passage about this for you. This would be a great Bible passage not only to read but to remember. It is Colossians 2:16–23.) They are very insistent that other people respect and admire them.

- They may refuse to accept responsibility for their decisions and actions, and for how those impact other people. "I was just being honest," they might say, when you thought it was rude and you saw how much it hurt the other person.

- They will seldom admit mistakes or sins. If they do, their confession will be designed to make them look even holier. Their usual course is to blame other people instead. They are not open to constructive criticism, and they may react strongly when they receive it.

- They will be arrogant. They won't be able to hide this because "the mouth speaks from the overflow of the heart" (Matthew 12:34). Listen to their talk, listen to see if their words, no matter how sugary, are condescending and judgmental.

If you see any of these, be suspicious. If you see two or more, run for the hills.

The Problem

So there's a problem—something between you and your goal.

Let's get at it by picturing a large meteor, a mile across and red hot, still at a distance but heading toward a small red convertible with leather seats and a first-rate sound system—the works. If the car isn't moved, it's toast. What do you do if you own the car?

Yep. You're going to jump in, put the pedal to the metal, and power your way out of there. The meteor can cause some damage, but it won't be to your little beauty.

The car is you.

God designed you to be beautiful and powerful. He also designed you to flee when the bad stuff is coming at you. If you get out of the way, you've got years of happy driving ahead of you. If you don't, it's squash city.

What is the meteor? It's a composite, a blend of new attractions, newly alive hormones, seductions from the movies and television and the Internet, temptations from other human beings, bad teaching, and bad thinking. It's being powered in your direction by enemies who do not love you. Enemies who would love to smash your life to pieces. Enemies that include the world's corrupt system, your own sinful desires, and, ultimately, Satan. And they will smash you. Unless you move.

That's your job right now—to take care of your beautiful life, to drive it out of harm's way and down the highway on a sunny day. Don't let the meteor wipe out your life.

Friends will tell you it's your life, that you can make your own choices—and they're right as rain. It is your life and nobody else's. It doesn't belong to your parents, so there's no use in living it just to please them or just to annoy them. It doesn't belong to your teachers, or the leaders at church, or your supervisor at work. It belongs to you, and you can make your own choices.

But many of these friends and others will tell you that you're free, and then do everything they can to get you to live *your* life *their* way. If you do it wrong, though, those people won't have to live with the consequences. Only you will. It's your life. The blessings of it are yours. And so are the calamities.

That's the problem.

The Deal

So you want to have fun. You see that God is for fun, but that you have to pay the price by making good decisions or it won't be fun for long. You want great relationships, but you know that no one is perfect and some people are really rotten. And God allows all of these people into your life, but He wants you to escape from a bunch of them. What's the deal here?

Well, here you are at the very start of your life—a young person with friendships and wonder and excitement stretching before you. Adventure and love await! But what you might not see clearly (because it's so hard to see) is that victory in personal relationship—the high point of love—lies just beyond the minefield of disaster.

The reward of a successful journey and good decision making—if marriage is for you—is someday finding and enjoying the love of a lifetime. But as with all great rewards, there is equivalent risk—a huge risk, a *monumental* risk, of making the biggest mistake you will ever make. Just like in a computer game, you've got to figure out how to get past the minefield.

And that's the deal. If you do it, if you get past the minefield, you can end up with great relationships and a great marriage. If you don't do it, you can end up with twisted and broken relationships and a very ugly marriage instead.

"I'm not ready to think about commitment and marriage," you might be saying. The problem is this: by the time you're ready, you might already be up to your elbows in commitment and marriage.

So what should you do?

You've got to be smart enough to take time. To learn about who you are. To find out who other people are—*really* are. To find out what kind of people celebrate you and what kind of people decimate you. To learn which people will liberate you and which people will dominate you.

If you take long enough to learn these things, you can get the best of the deal. You can make it past the minefield and not be shattered by explosive relationships. There's no magical age for knowing this, but you can be sure of one thing: No matter how smart you are, *it's not now.*

The Plan

Together we're going to win.

We're going to win by taking a very different approach to this crucial life decision. Instead of beginning with questions of dating and courtship, compatibility and relationship "tools," we're going to start with *you.*

Who have you become? Who are you becoming? Are you about to fall victim to one of the twelve lousy reasons to get married? Are you taking steps toward becoming a person worth marrying? In order to *find* the right person, you first have to *be* the right person.

Then, and only then, can you make sound decisions about the rest of your life.

Only then should you move to other questions and issues. Who is this other person? Who is she or he becoming? Are you about to fall into one of the twelve problems to avoid in getting married? Are you looking for the subtle clues that a person is really worth the risk of marrying? In order to find the right person, you have to know what "right" looks like. It's not as easy as it might seem. People can be attractive, intelligent, spiritual—and still not be good marriage partners if God is taking them in a different direction.

And then we'll go on to the most important questions of all—about the match itself. These questions may be mostly for later in your life, but it will be helpful if you have them floating around in the back of your mind even now.

So here they are. Even if you're ready and the other person is ready, does that automatically mean you're ready for *each other*? Have you really evaluated the "match"? Do you have all of the right reasons to get married in place? Have you thought through the twelve things to be sure of before you marry? Are you skilled in the ten secrets of knowing you've found *the one*?

In the last section of this book, we'll talk about what you do "in the meantime," while you're becoming and finding and evaluating. We'll talk about singleness and how to deal with sex.

Issues related to dating, courtship, and marriage are too complex to "sort out," at least very well, as you go along. Only the God who made us can give us the principles to make good decisions, and then make the good decisions "work." Only the One who created all of us single and invented marriage knows how to make it all work. And only dumb and unthinking people will try to do it without God.

I'm going to tell you the truth in this book. I bet you can handle it and keep reading and thinking. I'm here to bother and annoy you because I really want you to have it all. This is not possible unless you give up some of the bad ideas about marriage that you have picked up along the way.

Unfortunately, most adults won't tell us the truth. Why not? Well, it can be really hard to tell the truth. Some people just don't know it. Maybe they made it up as they went along, and now they're just trying to sort out the damage. Some may want you to live a life different than the one they lived, but they don't have the honesty and courage to tell you how they lived, and that *they* were seriously messed up at times (here's a truth—*everyone* has been seriously messed up at times). Some just want to "play God" and take control of your life.

And most of the books and other "help" out there won't help you, either. *Do date. Don't date. Have a courtship. Courtship is a relic of the past. Go find your soul mate. Don't do anything but wait; God will bring your mate to you. Marriage is the answer to your needs. You can't expect marriage to meet your needs. Love at first sight. Grow into love.* Pass the aspirin, please.

My goal is simple. I don't want you to avoid only poor marriages. I want you to avoid mediocre marriages as well. If you get married, my desire is that you have a great marriage. I'm going to tell it like it is because I want to help you think well and live with excellence. I will tell you the truth. But not all of it. Some, you'll have to dig out for yourself. Get ready to go on a quest for the truth about relationships.

To help you on your quest to discover the truth about great relationships, I have included some discussion questions at the end of each chapter. Of course, you may be reading this book for many reasons. You may be reading it on your own, as a youth group, with some friends, or with a person you are dating. My goal is to challenge you—whatever your situation—by giving you some specific questions to ponder or discuss. Those labeled "On Your Own" are questions to consider now, and again later, if you are thinking of dating a specific person. Those labeled "Together" are questions to discuss if you decide to date someone someday. Whatever the case, don't think of these as homework. Instead, consider them tools to help you become *the one*.

Discussion Questions

On Your Own

- *Ask Yourself:* What do I think "fun" is? Why? Why are relationships important?
- *Ask Your Parents:* What were the most fun relationships you had when you were my age? What made them fun? What would you change about how you related to the opposite sex? What are some clues to help me avoid dating the wrong person?
- *Ask Your Youth Pastor or Pastor:* Would you tell me three positive things you see in my closest friend(s)? Three negative things? Who in our youth group would you recommend that I keep at a distance? Why?

Together

- *Ask Each Other:* Here are some things I consider fun. Would you rate them on a one-to-ten scale? And would you tell me why?

By a series of flawless stratagems and carefully thought-out choices, she managed to marry the one person who thought she was both worthless and contemptible. She married a man who was happy to ratify her most negative assumptions and sentiments about herself, and who eventually came to hate everything about her.
Pat Conroy, in the novel *Beach Music*

becoming a person worth knowing and marrying

chapter 2

A lot of people are concerned about finding "The Right One." But that's starting at the wrong end of the equation.

To find The Right One, we first have to *become* The Right One. It's dumb to try to attract a great person if we're not at least trying to become a great person. If we've got great potential but haven't done anything to develop it, we're not likely to be considered a person worth knowing and marrying.

If you like to talk about ideas but you don't actually read and think, you'll have to settle for Erica, with her short attention span and desire to go out and party. If you like to be with and serve others but you don't volunteer to do these things, you'll end up with Jon, with

You must be before you can do or have.
Paul J. Meyer

his push to be alone with you and to spend the rest of the time on himself.

The bottom line is that you're not likely to attract someone a lot better than you. If you're a zero, the zeros will congregate around you like ants on an ice-cream sandwich. If you're lazy and slow-paced, you will not draw the attention of a hard-charging Renaissance person. If you don't read, no one who loves books and ideas will take you seriously.

It's the law of reaping and sowing: "Don't be deceived: God is not mocked. For whatever a man sows he will also reap" (Galatians 6:7).

If you sow superficiality, you will reap superficial friends. If you sow gossip and slander, you'll reap gossipy and hateful friends. If you sow nothing into your own development, you'll end up with shallow friends. You can't beat the principle. *Don't be misled*, we're told. Don't kid yourself. *Nothing* reaps . . . nothing.

But What If I Luck Out?

But what if you're lucky and manage to make a good *catch*? What if you're *really* lucky and manage to make a great catch— someone so far beyond where you are that you can't believe she is really interested in you? A few things are likely to occur.

- **Boredom.** Being an undeveloped twenty-five- or thirty-year-old is a formula for emptiness and depression. And even if your friend likes to teach, sooner or later he will get tired of being both his brain and yours.
- **Annoyance.** You'll get tired of her always teaching, lecturing, suggesting, encouraging, and pushing. And she will get frustrated having you as a deadweight chain around her ankles.
- **Regret.** You'll feel left out as he advances in his work and relationships and you don't (assuming you don't drag him down too far). He will regret being tied to someone who doesn't *get it* and who isn't a partner in anything but name.

- **Loneliness.** You'll always be on the outside of her serious friends. And she will feel limited in the kinds of things she can do with others because you will be an embarrassment. Feeling like you are out of the loop will leave you feeling more alone than you felt before you met her.

All in all, it's not a pretty picture. Even if you're *lucky*, you don't avoid the *reap-sow* principle. You just change the form of the reaping. Instead of drawing losers or mediocre people and suffering by having them around, you draw winners and ambitious people and cause them to suffer by having *you* around. Sooner or later, their misery caused by you will turn into your own misery caused by them.

So your options, if you're not planning to become a person worth knowing and marrying, are rather limited.

- You can be a marginal character who attracts other marginal characters; or
- You can be a marginal character who fools a going-somewhere person into thinking you're *not* a marginal character.

In either case, you still end up being a marginal character.

Are You Really Ready?

So here's the question: Are you *really* ready to be the kind of person who will be worth knowing?

Jake was taking a full load of classes and getting A's and B's in everything. He was on the school paper staff because that's where all of the really successful kids seemed to go in his school. He played keyboard in the youth worship band at church. He listened closely to the assistant youth pastor and tried to follow his example. He was strategizing on how to spend more time with Stephanie because she seemed to be the most serious Christian he knew. She was cute too.

All the teachers praised his efforts, but it didn't make him feel any better about himself. Some people told him his keyboard work was cool, but he always felt empty when they were gone and he was helping to break down the equipment. And Stephanie was keeping him at arm's length. She was friendly in a church-friendly sort of way, but that was it. *What gives?* he asked himself. *Shouldn't I feel better about my life?*

Jake is getting his feelings about himself from other people. He isn't really developing his own character. He's not letting the best of who he is and who he was designed to be come out. The activities he's involved in are fine in themselves, but he's deciding whether he is worthwhile based on who is praising him and how much. And now he is reaching out for Stephanie, in the futile hope that she will fill the emptiness. Jake isn't a bad guy. He just has a bad plan.

Jake has illusions about life and relationships.

So let's knock down some illusions and self-deception about this question of *readiness.*

Illusion #1: I know a lot of stuff because I'm doing well in school

People might have told you that your "job" right now is to go to school. So you go. You do at least most of the homework and a lot of the reading. You cram for tests.

But you can do all right in school and still not use it to advance the development of your own character. Do you ever think about what you're learning? Do you question it and challenge it? Do you offer your own ideas on what it all means or how it could be used? Do you listen to adults who might know one hundred times what you do on a topic? Do you understand why the chief technology officer of Microsoft once said that the main thing he studied to keep himself sharp was *history?*

School won't get the job done. Teachers can't give you character by osmosis. You can get a diploma and still have zero wisdom or street-smarts.

Illusion #2: I'm developing myself by spending a lot of time with the best people

You feel a pull toward the people who are accomplishing something. When possible, you spend time with them, go to their concerts or plays or other events, laugh at their jokes, and nod at their brilliant observations.

But you can spend time with geniuses and still be a tree stump. You can hang out with people who are building a Habitat for Humanity home and despise poor people. You can work shoulder-to-shoulder with Jesus for three years and sell Him out for chump change. Bad company might corrupt good character (see 1 Corinthians 15:33), but good company doesn't necessarily enhance bad character.

Other people's character won't automatically rub off on you. You can't become a person worth knowing just by *knowing* a person worth knowing.

Illusion #3: I attend a lot of church activities, so I'm bound to be with great people

You go to church every Sunday and other times as well. You seldom miss a youth group activity. You volunteer for all of the fund-raisers.

But you can go to church and be no better for the experience. You can attend to socialize and be accepted rather than to grow and become somebody special. You can let your mind wander to how beautiful she looks or how masculine he seems and miss the point of the activity. And some of the people present might be there to use and abuse rather than to give and forgive.

Church isn't exempt from bad guys. Wolves go to sheep pens. You can go to church and, if you're not paying attention, be with some of the most destructive people on earth.

Illusion #4: I'm trying to model myself after a great Christian so I can be great too

They talk about *quiet time,* and you've now built quiet times into your schedule—well, sort of. They do *daily devotionals,* and you're trying to get up early in the morning to follow their example. They said movies are evil and stopped going, and you're going to stop, too—well, right after that new Tom Cruise action flick with . . . what's her name?

The problem is that you can't copy your way to excellence. Imitation might be the sincerest form of flattery, but it makes you a *copycat,* not a winner. You can do quiet times and daily devotionals and Bible studies and camps and service work and *still* not be a person worth knowing. In fact, some of the people who do those things are so arrogant and insufferable that knowing them is a ticket to unhappiness. Copying them can lead to disaster.

Illusion #5: If I find the right friend, he will make me a better person

You feel the sin and the problems and the issues inside. You feel fragmented, like a toppled statue shattered on the ground. You're off your feet and feeling low. But that person seems willing to help! You know you can make it through if they pull you out!

Newsflash: No one can make you a better person. People can offer you advice and encouragement and help, and all of that is great. But none of it can make you do or be anything. I have poured my very best efforts into helping some young people (and adults) who *won't be helped,* no matter how much I love them or care about them. Most pastors, teachers, counselors, writers, speakers, older people, and younger people have experienced this. It can be disheartening, but it's the truth.

You don't need a friend to bail you out. You need to decide that you want to be something different, let God empower you, and start making changes. You need to give your expectations to God, not to other people. The old French proverb has it right: "The door to change is opened from the *inside.*" Other people can knock, but you have to open the door.

So here's the question again: Are you *really* ready to be the kind of person who will be worth knowing?

If not, are you ready to become that kind of person? Because if you are, the good news is this: You can do it.

Becoming the Right One

Becoming The Right One, a person worth knowing, is the first and most important place in which to spend your time and energies right now.

There is a sort of paradox here. If you spend your time trying to find the right person or people and live your life *out there,* you'll end up an empty shell. No one of quality will want to spend time with you.

On the other hand, if you spend your time discovering your God-given gifts and developing your strengths, you can end up with a rich character that will—almost as a by-product—draw some outstanding, genuine people to you.

This is also the only place where you have any control. Once you decide to live your life based on others' perceptions and approval, you have given them control of your life. You've turned over to them your heart, your feelings, and your sense of worth. You have disempowered yourself and empowered them. Some of them will take this power that you've given them and use it to hurt your soul.

There is an old saying that "to have a friend, you must first be a friend." At first reading, it looks like this is telling us to be friendly, which is certainly good advice. But take it deeper. What does *being a friend* really mean?

For some people, being a friend means spending time together, treating the other person nicely, trying not to hurt his feelings, loving him just as he is. It's doing things to get him to like you. It's like making a deal: *I'll treat you well if you'll do the same for me.* This is friendship as transaction. It's not all bad.

But much better than that, being a friend can mean becoming a person who changes the other person for the better just by being her friend. You spend your time developing your character (see Ephesians 4:2; Philippians 2:14), your relationship with God (see Mark 12:30), your relationship with yourself (see Mark 12:31), your ability to speak the truth in love (see Ephesians 4:15), and your genuine love for other human beings (see Romans 12:9–10). When you've done this, when you are really *being* a friend in the full sense of what that means, you are now offering something irresistibly juicy to every decent person who comes along.

Madison loved God. She loved to be with His people. Some of them were old and wise. Some were her parents' age, working out new ways to solve problems and change the world. Some were her age, funny, caring, excited about life. What she learned in these relationships gave her an ability to say just the right thing at just the right time. She sparkled with confidence and warmth and concern for others. Her reading filled her with interesting ideas. She had become the kind of person others wanted to know.

You want to become the best person you can possibly be because you know that in order to *find* the best person, you first need to *be* the best person.

When we're talking about "best," we're not talking about high self-esteem. The Bible has a different word for high self-esteem: *pride.* God says, "I tell everyone among you not to think of himself more highly than he should think. Instead, think sensibly" (Romans 12:3). What we're talking about is high self-*worth.* You are worth a lot—more than anything else in the universe. But it's because you're made in the image of God, reborn into his family, and remade in his image—not because you're hot.

We want God-esteem, not self-esteem. And who does God esteem? "He who is humble and contrite in spirit, and trembles at my word" (Isaiah 66:2b NIV). Someone who is like that is really hot—on fire for God.

When you focus on your own character, on doing something with the raw material that is *you*, you can get away from the need to get another person to puff you up and make you feel whole. You come to realize that a marriage partner is not a destination. He or she is a fellow pilgrim, heading with you to the destination. We have to prepare ourselves for an effective, loving joint pilgrimage.

Steps to Becoming a Person Worth Marrying

So let's say you really want to become a person worth knowing and marrying. How do you do it? What do you have to do—what do you have to *be*—in order to surround yourself with decent people?

Here are some steps you can take to become a person worth knowing and marrying.

Step #1: Become passionate about God. This is more than becoming a Christian or going to church or Bible study. This means making God the center of your life. The alternative is that you try to make other people the center of your life, with a potential spouse your bull's-eye. Or worse, you could make *you* the center of your life, and you're just too little to be God. But someone is going to be in the center—if not God, somebody. You are not ready to be married until God is in the center and you are already intimate with Him. In spite of popular ideas to the contrary, marriage by itself is not likely to bring you closer to God. If you develop a unique, passionate relationship with the living God, He will bless you richly in your life and relationships, and you will become attractive to people who think their own souls are also valuable.

Step #2: Know the truth. Babies don't get married, and baby Christians shouldn't either. You certainly don't want to get married if you're not a Christian. Life is hard enough without trying to do marriage on your own. But you also don't want to get married until you've grown up a little in Christ. *Quite* a little. It's what you know about life through God's lens that makes all the difference. Do you know the truth? Do you love it? Do you know that perception isn't reality? Are you aware of where you are reality-impaired and need a strong dose of truth to get well? Are you ready to lay aside the illusions, including common "Christian" illusions? Most people don't really want to know the truth unless it is pleasant. You can be one of a kind. You can want to know all of it. If you know the truth—really know it and love it and believe it—"you will become free" (John 8:32).

Step #3: Live in freedom. Even if you know the truth, are you really free? Do you really believe and experience the fullness of the truth that "Christ has liberated us into freedom" (Galatians 5:1)? Are you living in freedom—free of the power and plague of sin, free to say "no" to temptation, free to think for yourself, free of the always-lurking Christian Pharisees and their petty rules? Most people aren't free. Someone who walks in freedom will be attractive to anyone else who wants to be free. You weren't put here to place people in the bondage of a bad relationship. You were put here "to proclaim freedom for the captives" (Isaiah 61:1 NIV).

Step #4: Become passionate about others. People talk about crowns in heaven. Do you know what they are? According to the Bible, your crowns are *other people.*[1] Are you spending yourself in service to others? Are you investing in others? Is the world around you—at home, at work, at school, at church, in the community—at least a little better because of your drive to make it so? Are you practicing on your parents and siblings, who can probably be rather unlovable at times? Even if you have a lot of head knowledge about the Bible, do you have the heart knowledge that goes with it? Do you know that "knowledge inflates with pride, but love builds up" (1 Corinthians 8:1)? If you don't have the humility to "consider others better than yourselves,"[2] you're not ready for serious relationship. Most people who get married don't have that humility, so their relationships are all about rights and resentment. You can do a lot better than that.

Step #5: Become passionate about your responsibilities. Mark Twain said, "I never let my schooling interfere with my education." Are you pouring yourself into your studies, both in school *and otherwise,* so you can say, like the people said to Nehemiah, "We assume the responsibility" (Nehemiah 10:32 NIV)? Are you looking for the work and career that will resonate with your soul?[3] Have you refused to absorb the lies, like the idea about "full-time Christian work" (if you're a Christian, all work is), and "I'm just working to get money so I can serve God" (the work is a big part of your service; see Colossians 3:17), and "it's not all supposed to be enjoyable—that's why they call it work" (joy is a choice, not just an emotion)?[4] Have you learned that your work can be an expression of the best that is in you? If you're waiting for teachers or parents or bosses or friends to give you a push on your responsibility, you're ready for training, not serious relationship. God wants you to "be diligent in these matters; give yourself wholly to them, so that everyone may see your progress."[5]

Step #6: Find a greater cause. Have you found something bigger than yourself that you can devote yourself to? Have you at least made a stab at the questions about impact ("what am I here to change?"), significance ("what am I here to build?"), and legacy ("what do I want to leave behind—when I graduate? when I leave my first job? when I die?")? Are you certain that the daily drumbeat of life and the friction and demands of relationships won't take you off your deepest reasons for being here? These reasons can change or blossom over time, but if you want to be someone special, someone whose life counts for something, the time to start is *now*—not after high school or college, at some unidentified time down the road when you're older. If you don't have some outstanding reason to be here, your life will be too insignificant to have any outstanding relationships.[6]

Step #7: Learn the power of redemption. Have you learned how to make a comeback? Have you learned that mistakes aren't fatal, that you can learn and grow and improve, that failure comes from quitting rather than from making mistakes? Do you know forgiveness—how to experience it *and* how to grant it? Do you cut people slack when they foul up? Are you a person of the "second chance"? Have you learned how to *meet in the middle?*[7]

Relationships are about failure and redemption. Many people don't know how to fail and come back. They hide when they make mistakes and pout and hold grudges when they're hurt. And most people don't know how to let others fail and come back. They can't make themselves apologize when they've caused the problem, and they can't forgive when the other person has messed up big-time. If you don't know and practice the power of redemption, you will never be able to build a serious relationship with another complex and fragile human being.

If you can work on these seven powerful steps, you will indeed become a person worth knowing and marrying. You don't do it to find a marriage partner, though. You do it to find a life.

But here's some exciting news: If you become this type of person, you stand a good chance of being interesting to a person of the opposite sex who is becoming the same kind of person.

Get out of the way, world!

Jennie's Story

Jennie finally got it.

She had been working hard all through middle school and most of high school to get a lot of people to like her. She had laughed at jokes that weren't funny, gone to parties that were boring, and spent time with people who were shallow and uninteresting. She tried to adapt and become what other people wanted her to be, like Julia Roberts' character in *The Runaway Bride.* She had thought this was what Paul meant in the Bible when he said, "I have become all things to all men."[8]

But none of it worked. She didn't have any close friends, except maybe for Janelle. She didn't even like Janelle that much. All she wanted to do was talk about music. It felt like most of the other people Jennie had spent time with were just tolerating and humoring her.

Then she took the step. After a Bible study on the seven steps to becoming a person worth knowing, she decided to stop worrying about what other people thought. She decided to make herself into someone special with God's help. Someone who was passionate about God and people and life and learning and work. Someone who knew how to walk in truth and freedom. Someone who dared to make a difference. She decided to take Paul's advice to young Timothy: "No one should despise your youth; instead, you should be an example to the believers in speech, in conduct, in love, in faith, in purity" (1 Timothy 4:12).

The results weren't immediate. In fact, the first result hurt. Janelle decided she was weird and pulled away. But Jennie persisted. And then, slowly, things around her began to change. She found herself doing things with people who were really serious about life and who were really interesting. She found herself in conversations with passionate people who were trying to figure out how to make their lives count. She saw that she couldn't change other people. But she could change herself, and slowly other people were changing in response to the change they saw in her.

She started feeling good about her life. In fact, for the first time, Jennie felt like she really *had* a life.

Jennie discovered a sobering truth that few people ever really get—that life *around* us doesn't change until we change the life that is *within* us. But Jennie finally got it.

You can get it, too.

Discussion Questions

On Your Own

- *Ask Yourself:* What three things am I doing right now that are helping me become a person worth knowing? How will the world be different in three years because of me? What am I doing to grow in _____ (one of the seven steps)?

- *Ask Your Parents:* Without being too critical, could you point out ways you think I could grow in each of the seven steps given in this chapter? (Let your parents read them if they haven't already.)

- *Ask Your Youth Pastor or Pastor:* What illusions do you think I might have about my own spiritual or psychological development? Could we do a study in our youth group on each of the seven steps in this chapter to learn how to practice them?

Together

- *Ask Each Other:* Pick one of the seven steps in this chapter each week and talk about what you're doing to grow in that area. Talk about your frustrations and failures in trying to practice this step.

All marriages are happy.
It's the living together afterward that causes all the trouble.
Raymond Hull

recognizing a person worth knowing and marrying

chapter 3

King Solomon said and did some astonishing things, but when it came to thinking about people he was sort of negative: "While I was still searching but not finding—I found one upright man among a thousand, but not one upright woman among them all" (Ecclesiastes 7:28 NIV).

Those are not very good odds. If you're a girl, that's one-tenth of one percent. I guess Solomon is saying that *at least you've got a chance.* But if you're a guy, well . . .

Seriously, what Solomon is getting at is that finding a person worth knowing is a tough assignment. All people deserve our respect, at least until they've earned our disrespect. But that

> *The LORD looks down from heaven*
> *on the sons of men*
> *to see if there are any who understand,*
> *any who seek God.*
> **Psalm 14:2 NIV**

doesn't mean that all people are worth large amounts of our time, our hearts, or our advice.

Not every person is a worthy marriage partner. And God wants only the very best for you.

Are They Really Ready?

The Bible tells us that "a righteous man is cautious in friendship" (Proverbs 12:26 NIV).

Since we've put *knowing* ahead of *marrying,* this is telling us to be very careful whom we know. There are so many bad choices for friends—some of them bad for anybody, some of them just bad for *you.*

I've heard people say, "Don't date anyone you wouldn't be willing to marry." That's a little silly, since you can't even know most people until you spend some time with them. The advice should actually start earlier in the game: "Don't date anyone you wouldn't be willing to have as your friend." Let friendship be your test, your barrier, your wall. Be friendly to all, but friends only with a few.

You want to make sure that you are cautious in friendship. Take your time. Spend enough time to see if there is anything there for you. If not, don't waste your investment of yourself. Move on. If you sense that a person could be a real friend, move ahead—slowly. Out of the people you have as real friends, close friends, some will be of the same sex. Don't lose these people because you're focused on a friend of the opposite sex. Good friends are too hard to come by and too easy to lose through neglect.

So let's say you've come to see that a close friend of the opposite sex is stirring more than friendship feelings in you. How will you know if those feelings mean something good? What should you look for to know that the person won't turn from a good friend to a bad partner? How will you know that you are not about to wreck a good friendship for a lousy romance?

In this chapter, we will look at seven strong clues that will help you make an honest assessment of the marriage-readiness of another person.

But first, we'll have to knock down some illusions.

Illusion #1: A person's focus on himself is only natural, and this will fade as he gets older

Todd really liked Nicole, and they had been dating seriously for more than a year. He thought she had a lot of positive qualities, but he was getting more and more turned off by her focus on her appearance. She'd be an hour late because she was doing something with her hair. She was having "make-overs"—whatever those were—all the time. She was always shopping for clothes, and hating wearing the same thing more than once or twice. When he talked about it with one of his male friends, they both felt clueless. "Girls just like to look good," his friend said. "Don't get bent out of shape. Just enjoy how good she looks." Todd smiled, but wasn't sure he bought it.

A lot of people say that teenagers and young adults are "naturally" self-centered. I don't buy that. I think some people always put themselves first because they're *sinners*, not because they're a certain age.

Self-focus is not as likely to *fade* as it is to get *worse*. Don't think you'll get a person like this to think about others very easily. God has already been working on him or her for years!

Illusion #2: People who are responsible in school will be responsible in work, marriage, and parenting

Stephen really impressed Kari with his study habits. He was always reading, working on a project, or cramming. "Now this is the kind of guy who'll be a good husband and father," she thought. Kari was already picturing herself standing in the kitchen of her future home.

Stephen might be responsible about school for many different reasons, some of them not that great. Maybe he's getting pressure from his parents. He may lose some of his privileges or even get grounded if he doesn't keep his grades at a certain level. Perhaps he's just hypercompetitive, and wants to get a better grade than others. Maybe he's just trying to impress Kari. She needs to find out the *why* of Stephen's effort, not just the *what*.

Illusion #3: Clean-cut and sharp on the outside means decent on the inside

Alex thought Shonna looked like an angel. She was like Jennifer Aniston in *Friends*. She looked like that girl-next-door figure-skating champion. She came across like Britney Spears without the attitude. Shonna was *it*. He'd dated her for two months, and it was already feeling like heaven. He wanted to be serious about a girl who was solid gold to the core. But Alex didn't know that innocence was not on Shonna's wish list. She had already been involved sexually three times, and she loved talking with her friends about "how it was" with those guys.

Alex was about to find out that Shonna was gold—but not to the core. She didn't need a ring from Alex because she already *was* a ring. "Like a gold ring in a pig's snout," the Bible says, "is a beautiful woman who shows no discretion" (Proverbs 11:22 NIV).

You will never know what a person is like—gold in the soul or gold in the pig's nose—until you get past outward appearances and get down to character. There is nothing more common in the world than attractive, beautiful, or gorgeous people who are ugly inside.

Illusion #4: If he's spending a lot of time with me, he must think I'm really special

Brandon called Cassie every night. They would talk while doing their homework, or listening to music, whatever. He would read her poetry, some of which he'd written, which she thought was so cool. They were out together at all of the school parties, plays, concerts, and sporting events. Brandon had taken her by storm. A few months ago, she only knew him as a fellow student in two classes. Now she couldn't imagine life without him.

What Cassie *doesn't* know is about to hurt her. Brandon is focused on a goal, and that's to have sex with her. He's gotten hooked on Internet porn, but it's no longer giving him the same "high" that it used to. He wants to try it out with someone. He *intends* to try it out—with Cassie. He just knows that the way to get to her will take some time and work.

People can spend time—lots of time—with you for all sorts of reasons. They might not want to think for themselves. They may be too lazy to build other friendships. They might be trying to fix their own desperate loneliness by filling up all of their time with you. Don't fall for this illusion. Time could be a blessing—or time could be a trap.

Illusion #5: We've never had a fight, so we must be in harmony

Lauren and Nate were on cloud nine. They'd been dating for seven months, and they were already bragging to their friends that they always got along, no matter what.

This might be harmony—or it might be the calm before the storm. Lauren and Nate could be in the eye of a hurricane. This apparent harmony could be a king-sized deception. Maybe they're not fighting because they haven't really talked about anything important. They could be dodging everything that might be a little thorny. Perhaps they're pretending to be in a dream world, where people who love each other don't fight—a world that doesn't exist in any marriage.

And harmony is oversold, anyway. The Bible is into *friction* at least as much as it is into harmony.[1] Maybe there's no fighting for a bad reason: *Maybe they just don't care.*

Here's one last thing to think about on this harmony business. People will never treat you nicer than they will before they've got you hooked. What if this is the best it will ever be? What if it's all heading downhill from here?

Finding "The Right One"

Most people have no clear idea of what The Right One would look like, even if they saw her. The result is that we walk through life with vague ideas of what would complete us or help us be successful, without really knowing what that is. Sometimes we get distracted by physical attraction, which can fade with time.

The real question is, *What character traits will stand the test of time?*

In this section, we want to take a little time to define what The Right One might be, by helping you think through what is important to you based on biblical principles, your own spirit and personality, your experience, and the wisdom of others.

Biblical Principles. When Jesus was telling a story about someone inviting people to a great banquet—the Someone was God—one person turned down the invitation with this excuse: "I just got married, so I can't come" (see Luke 14:20). Marriage can be a great thing, but it is a lousy substitute for an invitation from God. Is the person you are interested in more focused on the Lord than on you? You're too little to be his god, so you'd better make sure that you haven't taken the job. When Paul was encouraging people on how to live without concerns, he made the startling statement that "from now on those who have wives should be as though they had none" (1 Corinthians 7:29b). Is he telling us that Christians can pretend that they don't have spouses? No. He's just saying that the marriage had better not take the place of living "so that you may be devoted to the Lord without distraction" (1 Corinthians 7:35b).

Your Spirit and Personality. Each of us is wired differently. Most friendships can survive major personality differences, but it's a lot harder in a marriage. With a friendship, you can always go home and not return your friends' calls for a few days. With a marriage, when you go home your spouse is *there.* If you're an optimist who thinks the glass is half full and your spouse's a pessimist who thinks it's half empty, your marriage might break the glass. If you're focused on possibilities and are willing to take risks, and she is focused on limitations and hates feeling insecure, a mix might produce a lot of collateral damage. If you enjoy time alone and she wants to do everything together, warning, warning! If you want to have a lot of children and he isn't so hot on kids, he probably won't enjoy it more when he's changing a dirty diaper at 2:00 A.M. Make sure you know who you are, what you like, and what you can't stand. Then choose an intimate friend accordingly. (We'll cover this in more detail in chaps. 8–10.)

Your Experience. Use your experience with this person now in the small things to get some idea of what your experience with him will be like later in the big things. For example, what if you have no "margin of error" with him? What if any mistake you make—like being late, disagreeing with him in front of others, or forgetting to do something he asked you to do—leaves you feeling like you could lose him if you're not careful? What if he tells you he forgives you, but in the middle of a conversation three months later something triggers him to bring it all back up again? Do you really want to live the rest of your life with no margin, feeling like you're on the edge of a relational cliff?

Another clue is his parents. Have you had some less-than-pleasant encounters with his father? With his mother? Be street-smart enough to know that your friend *will* become like his parents in at least many ways—no matter what he looks like or seems like now.

The Wisdom of Others. Get a lot of input from people who know your friend. Ask them for their observations, questions, concerns, doubts, and fears. If you don't ask, a lot of people won't tell you. Or they'll tell you only the positive things, because they think that's what you want to hear and they don't want to hurt you or lose your friendship. Try to plan yourselves into a lot of things with your other friends—not just because there is safety in numbers (there is), but because it will give them a lot of chances to see you and your friend in action.

You can also gain wisdom by reading books—good books that don't play games with your life. You can discuss this book with your friends, parents, pastors, and teachers. And you can use the wisdom that people have built into personality profiling and testing, not as a magical compatibility bullet, but as a way of knowing yourself and the other person, and of seeing whether you have a chance of having a good marriage.

Take a few minutes now, or as soon as you can, to sit down and decide what is important to you in another person. You could title the page *Here's what the right person will be like,* and make it as real and serious as you can. Leave some room to add some more thoughts as you read the important stuff in the rest of this chapter.

Clues to Finding a Person Worth Marrying

So let's say you really want to find a person worth knowing and marrying. How do you do it? What do you need to do in order to identify him or her?

What are the clues that a person might be worth marrying? There are seven key character traits to look for.[2]

Clue #1: Purity. Does this person really know what God means by the word *purity*? This word can be used in either a *holier-than-thou* or a *hokier-than-thou* kind of way. But real purity is neither one. Real purity isn't *better-than-you* kind of thinking. And it isn't *life-is-so-sweet* kind of thinking either. Real purity is hard-earned. It isn't prudish and judgmental. It doesn't throw out an entire book or movie because of a word or phrase. But it also doesn't pretend that nasty words and scenes don't have a negative impact. Is this person bothered by *anything*? Is she bothered by *everything*? If the answer is no to the first question or yes to the second, you've got your clues. Move on.

Clue #2: Peace-loving. We're told to "be of the same mind, be at peace" (2 Corinthians 13:11). You can't be of one mind if you're not living in peace. Make sure that your friend is pursuing "peace with everyone" (Hebrews 12:14). Does he try to do what "promotes peace" (Romans 14:19)? As far as it depends on him, does he "live at peace with everyone" (Romans 12:18)? How does he react when people correct him? Or rebuke him? Or instruct him and teach him? Proverbs 9:7–9 gives you a whole bunch of things to look for. If he insults someone who corrects him, what is he? If he abuses someone who rebukes him, what is he? And if he listens to instruction and teaching, what is he? Responses are full of good leads. "God has called you to peace," we're told (1 Corinthians 7:15). Make sure your friend has this fruit of the spirit (see Galatians 5:22–23). A marriage needs a justice of the peace—the Prince of Peace.

Clue #3: Considerate (or gentle at all times). Does she really know how to be a friend? Does she put the interests of others—not just you, but *others*—ahead of her own? In part, being considerate means finding out what the other person needs from you. For example, the Bible says, "Each one of you is to love his wife as himself, and the wife is to respect her husband" (Ephesians 5:33). Why would the apostle Paul command these things in this passage? *Because they don't come naturally!*

You can do some advance checking by asking yourself, if you're a young woman, "Does he really love me like he loves himself? Here's what he does for himself—does he do that for me?" If you're a young man, you can ask yourself, "Does she really respect me? Or is it obvious from her comments and the way she treats me that she doesn't hold me in high regard." No marriage can survive a man without respect or a woman without love. Now is the time to find out if these—and other—things are there. This word can also mean "gentle." Does she let her "graciousness be known to everyone" (Philippians 4:5)?

Clue #4: Submissive (or compliant or willing to yield to others). Do you detect any real humility? When she prays, do you sense honesty and humility and true brokenness? Is he willing to give-and-take on what you do or where you go? If he won't give you the remote control or get off the computer, or she won't let you hang out with the guys, take notice. Does your friend ever let other people have their way, even when you know it isn't your friend's top choice? Does he listen when you and others talk (we can be fooled into thinking that because he has ears he is listening!)? Is he overly critical of your friends? Does she encourage you to be involved with other people and work on projects with others? If she tries to keep you away from people or work that you're interested in, you can bet she'll stifle your relationships and ministry after you're married.

Does he ignite the Spirit's fire in you—or does he stifle it (see 1 Thessalonians 5:19)? If he uses a bucket now, he'll use a fire hose then. Make sure you watch how he treats you around others—and how he treats others around you. And if she wants to be in control (she insists on picking the movie) but doesn't want to take any responsibility if things don't work out (she refuses to acknowledge that she ignored a lot of advice about the movie), buckle your seat belt and get ready for a ride over which *you* will have no control.

Clue #5: Full of mercy and good fruit (or good deeds). Unlike judgmental people, this person will sometimes say *I understand* when someone sins or makes a huge mistake. And these people don't give until it hurts; they give until it *feels good.* One of the things that is always on their minds is to do something—write something, finish a project, help someone, make something happen. If he says, "I'm too young to do very much" or "You can't expect that much from me right now," you have your clue. He's void of good deeds. Does he gladly take on responsibility (volunteer to help with clean-up or put away chairs), or does he wait for someone else to do it? It might be that he's avoiding responsibility because he's lazy, or it may be because he's afraid of failure. The reason won't matter to you if you get very involved with him. You'll just feel very, very stuck.

Clue #6: Impartial (or shows no partiality, or without favoritism). Amy knew the truth, and she knew that Jordan was aware of it, too. She was the one who was supposed to tell the four people who hadn't come about the party. She felt awful about it. But when Kelsey said she was sure that Heather was supposed to make those calls, Jordan was all over it. He agreed that it must have been the absent Heather who had blown it. Amy felt relief, and she felt good about Jordan standing up for her like that. Should she feel that way? Or should she be concerned that Jordan was favoring her over Heather and—even worse—favoring her feelings over the truth?

You don't want to be too close to a person who plays favorites, forms little cliques, or puts down people who aren't part of *the group.* You also want to be on guard about someone who wants you to spend all of your best efforts and time on her, to the exclusion of your other friends. You don't want to be her "favorite," if being that means that she has a right to be jealous or can act like she owns you. You want a relationship that's savory, not slavery.

Clue #7: Sincere (or without hypocrisy). Is he genuinely interested in your becoming all that God designed you to be? Or is his real interest in you becoming all that *he* wants you to be? Is he genuine when he tells you how he feels? Or does he use manipulation, nagging, or complaining—done in the name of "love"—to get his needs met? And if he's pressing you to meet all of his needs, you can end up feeling inadequate when you don't meet them (you can't meet them all), but also jealous about anyone who *can* meet some of the needs you can't.

If your friend scores high to very high on each of these critical character traits, you've got a very good friend indeed. Remember that it takes time to give an accurate grade. And over time, if all else fits—if you've both got the best reasons to marry (see chap. 8), if you're both sure of some very important things (see chap. 9), and if you both know that the other is *the one* (see chap. 10)—you might have the love of your life.

But if he or she scores low or very low on even one of these traits, this person may not be worth *knowing* any deeper. A person like this is most certainly *not* worth marrying.

Kyle's Story

You've done some pretty dumb things, Kyle told himself as he looked up at the ceiling of his bedroom. He had his hands folded behind his head on the pillow, and he let his eyes focus on the light streaming in from the tall, open window.

You've done some pretty dumb things, but this time you've gone too far. He had been going out seriously with Macy since the start of their senior year. She was a very nice girl in many ways and was certainly attractive. They had even talked about going to the same college together and had discussed engagement a couple of times when they were out alone.

This is getting way too serious, he thought as he propped himself up in bed. What bothered him was Macy's willingness to have a fight over . . . nothing. They'd go out a couple of times without a problem, and then—boom! He'd try to think about it afterward and to figure out what he'd said or done, but sometimes there just seemed to be no good reason.

The kicker was being around her mother. Macy and her mother fought constantly, over everything and over nothing. He was beginning to see that it was her way of life. *She just doesn't understand how to get along with people,* he thought. When he asked Pastor Tim about it last night, Tim tried to be diplomatic but ended up saying that anyone marrying Macy would be living in a war zone for the rest of his life. They'd looked together at some verses on "peace." None of them seemed to fit Macy.

That's it! He said as he slowly stood up. He knew she wasn't safe, not even as a friend. It would be hard to break it off. But Kyle's mind was made up.

There would be no disasters in his life, if he had anything to say about it.

Discussion Questions

On Your Own

- *Ask Yourself:* Do I have the seven traits listed in James 3:17? How do I know? If not, what will I change? Do my friends have each of these traits? How do I know?

- *Ask Your Friend(s):* Do I have the seven traits listed in James 3:17? How do you know? Do you have each of these traits? (You might want to compare your friends' evaluations with your own evaluation. Share with each other the weaknesses you discovered. Discuss how these weaknesses might affect the people around you.)

- *Ask Your Parents:* What traits do you think are important in a friend or possible spouse? What would your make-it-or-break-it character trait be?

- *Ask Your Youth Pastor or Pastor:* Would you score my friend(s) and me on a one-to-ten scale on each of the seven clues? Would you be very specific in telling us your reasons for any low ratings?

Together

- *Ask Each Other:* (Discuss each of the seven clues and evaluate each other against these clues.) Where do you think you are weak in being considerate (or one of the other seven clues)? How does this compare with what I said about you? How can you improve in the weak areas? How can I improve in the weak areas?

- *Ask Your Youth Pastor or Pastor:* Would you score each of us on a one-to-ten scale on each of the seven clues? Would you be very specific in telling us your reasons for any low ratings?

By obedience to the truth, having purified yourselves . . .
love one another earnestly from a pure heart.
1 Peter 1:22

kissing dumb dating good-bye

chapter 4

Your biggest challenge isn't to kiss dating good-bye. It's to kiss *disaster* good-bye.

What is disaster? Many people will tell you that you can end up in all kinds of trouble—premarital sex, disease, pregnancy, shame, and disgrace. Certainly, all of those dangers are there. Because of them, a lot of leaders and teachers will tell you that all dating is wrong. They treat the idea of young people out together as a potential nuclear meltdown that must be avoided at all costs.

But there are other kinds of disaster that are less obvious but no less destructive. This is where you get involved emotionally well beyond your willingness or ability to make real commitments. It's where you put yourself in a position to make promises that you aren't really sure you want to make. It's where you're treating each other like Hollywood stars,

Flee from youthful passions, and pursue righteousness, faith, love, and peace, along with those who call on the Lord from a pure heart.
2 Timothy 2:22

and you're not even sure you know this other person that well, or like who he or she is.

Dumb dating is about making yourself and another person the center of the universe (fortunately, that job is already taken by God). A lot of people think it's cool to go out on that "one-on-one" kind of time together, where you focus on each other. Just the two of you. Feels so mature, so "adult," so independent, so *free*.

But not you, because you're smarter than that. You know that if it's all about you, it's all about illusion. You want to see how this guy treats you around other people. You want to see if she's interested in others or only in herself and the extension of herself (that's you). *You want to see if this other person has a shred of decency or generosity or humility or gentleness.*

So when you date—which we'll define in a minute—you do it intelligently. You use it as an opportunity to love someone "earnestly from a pure heart." You use it as a vehicle to find "faith, love, and peace." You use it as a chance to enjoy companionship with people of good will. *And you use it as an opportunity to improve your character and the character of another person, rather than a chance to use that individual.* There's no other way to do these things than in the real world.

So dating isn't the issue. Dumb, reckless, unbiblical dating is the issue.

What Is Dating?

Let's start by listing everything the Bible says about dating:

Well, that was easy. Here's something most people won't tell you about dating: The Bible doesn't include it as a topic. It just isn't there.

Now, there are *principles* that apply to doing everything in life, including dating. So let's talk about dating from the perspective of a few of those principles.

Dating is developing a relationship with a human being made in the image of God, a human being whom He created and for whom He died. It is about *companionship*. These people we date aren't "practice" relationships. They are real relationships, with real human beings, who will be changed forever because of the time they spend with us. For good or bad.

Young single adults have every bit as much need and right to have solid relationships as older or married people do. You were created for relationships with God and other people. You have every reason to hope that those relationships will be satisfying and effective.

Dating is about getting to know people, including yourself. It is different from parent-child, spouse-spouse, or sibling relationships. By dating, you are not committing to get engaged or get married, or even the possibility of those things, unless you are exceedingly naïve or just plain dumb. *Many Christians don't realize that dating isn't "courtship" or "matchmaking."* One recent article in a Christian magazine was subtitled "Online Matchmaking Is Changing the Christian Dating Game."[1] There is more wrong with this subtitle than we could possibly hope to cover in less than a hundred pages. But let's say simply that surfing the web for a marriage partner is like looking through a garbage can for a ham sandwich. And dating is not a "game"—it's about developing relationships.

We are told to be "considerate" (Titus 3:2), "completely humble and gentle" (Ephesians 4:2), and to think of others "more highly" (Romans 12:3) than ourselves. These principles are not suspended during dating. The Golden Rule, to treat others in only the way you would want them to treat you, applies also to dating. The second greatest commandment, to love this person as you love yourself, is in full force.

If we cause someone to stumble, Jesus stated that it would be better if we had a heavy millstone tied around our necks and were thrown, Mafia-style, into the water to drown (Matthew 18:6; Mark 9:42; Luke 17:2). *If you're not sure how to avoid making this other person stumble, you're not ready to date that individual.*

We're supposed to serve others, welcome strangers, and care especially about the family of God. This means that dating can never be used as an excuse not to do these things. In fact, people who are on the right track will use their relationship to bless others. Elitism and cliquishness and exclusiveness are out of place, and couples who do it are showing that they are too immature to be dating.

Think about what you've learned about God and the Bible. What other general biblical principles would apply to dating? When we've got these crucial principles in mind, we can relate to other people with integrity *and* intensity.

Smart Dating

Let's talk about smart dating, about knowing when and how to participate.

In the first place, smart dating is about *friendship.* "Dating" at its best is really another way of saying, "meeting and getting to know people." This means that to date intelligently we have to know how to be good friends. We have to know how to choose friends, build friendships, and end friendships that are destructive.

If you think of dating as a friendship adventure rather than a romantic adventure, you're more likely to end up with many friends—and someday, perhaps, real romance.

Choosing Friends

We often wipe ourselves out at the start by picking the wrong people as friends. Stay away from mean and nasty people, no matter how talented or popular they may be. Recognize that we are often drawn to people who are in emotional pain like we are. This is a lot like two alcoholics trying to help each other stay sober—it's not likely to work very well.

After you meet a person and are getting to know him, go over the "Twelve Problem People to Avoid" in chapter 7. If you think this person may be one of these "Problem People," keep your distance. If these problems are really glaring, move along. God doesn't require you to spend time with everyone who comes along. In fact, God tells us to avoid contact with certain kinds of people. Look up these words in a concordance: "Keep away; stay away; avoid; flee."

Keys to Building Great Friendships

Here are a few suggestions on building great friendships (they apply to all friendships, not just dating friendships):

Key #1: Tell each other the truth at all times. You can't have a great friendship based on a lie. If you have certain subjects that are "taboo" or off limits, if she reacts strongly against your attempts to tell her the truth, if she works hard to avoid facing reality, you have little foundation for a friendship.

Key #2: Be interested in his life before yours. When you meet with a friend, come prepared to ask him about his life and to show genuine interest. Too many friendships are focused on *telling* rather than *listening*.

Key #3: Make sure there is mutual commitment. You can have a friendship of sorts with someone where you are giving 70 percent and she is giving 30 percent, but it isn't a great friendship. When you sense that your friend is not as interested in calling you as you are in calling her, when you feel that you are wanting to be with her more than she is with you, it's time to regroup. Either you need to talk with her and find out what is holding her back, or you need to back off until her commitment makes it to your level. There is truth in the old saying, "To have a friend, you must first be a friend," but to have a great friend, she has to want it as much as you do.

Key #4: Share values and mutual trust. You can love many people, but you can't be close friends with someone who doesn't share your core values. This is the basis of trust. Great friendships have high levels of trust both ways, because both people believe deeply in the same important principles.

Key #5: Make freedom a top priority. We are told, "Christ has liberated us into freedom. . . . don't submit again to a yoke of slavery" (Galatians 5:1). Great friends do more than *allow* you to be free; they *insist* that you be free. When the other person tries to make you feel guilty if you're not spending time with him, when he tries to have everything his way, you can be sure that a "yoke of slavery" is not far away. You don't own your friend and he doesn't own you. God has prior claim on both of you.

Key #6: Find a way to serve your friend. Everyone needs help in some way, whether it's encouragement about a tough teacher or class, advice about a difficult parent, or aid in studying a challenging subject. Service has an amazing effect on human relationships.

Key #7: Find a way to challenge your friend. Great friends challenge each other to grow, to make a difference, to be great for God. A friend makes you feel big, not small. She helps you see the possibilities, not just the limitations. She helps you believe you can do things that a month ago seemed a hundred miles beyond your reach. Great friends don't love you "just as you are" (another myth); they love the whole you, including the "you" that has a touch of greatness, the "you" that you can't even see.

Key #8: Show gratitude and appreciation. Human beings can be ungrateful and unappreciative. Great friends are thankful for you. They appreciate everything, including the little things. They don't take you for granted, or expect you to do something for them because you're their friend and it's your "job." And they cheer the loudest when you achieve something or do something well.

Key #9: Involve others in your friendship. Other people are like vitamins and minerals to help you build a healthy friendship (some are like fertilizer). You get to see how other people respond to your friend. You get to see how he treats you around others. You get to see how she treats others around you. If there is real love in your relationship, there should be enough to spill over onto others.

Key #10: Be open to criticism about the relationship from others. Friendships formed in a vacuum can develop all sorts of unhealthy attributes. You need the observations, insight, wisdom, and warnings of other people. You have to be careful, of course, that this criticism isn't driven by jealousy or some other wrong motive. Even parents can sometimes have a breathtaking insight for you, if you're smart enough to listen.

Ending Friendships

One of the hardest things to do in life is to end a relationship. Ending one can make us feel like we've wasted our time, or that we're a failure, or that we're being "unchristian." But if we don't learn how to do this, we will end up with lousy friends and less-than-ideal dates, and probably a messed-up life.

How do you know when to end a friendship?

- **First,** go back to your original choice and evaluate honestly whether you should have gotten involved with this person in the first place.

- **Second,** go over the "Keys to Building Great Friendships" information above and ask "Does this person ever do any of these things with me?" If not, or if he makes just token efforts, it's time to hit the road and put him in your rearview mirror.

- **Third,** review the "Twelve Problem People to Avoid" in chapter 7. If you see any of these traits in your friend, have the smarts and courage to move along. Don't be friends with—and certainly don't marry—anyone who makes your stomach churn.[2] In the words of Mike Murdock, "Go where you are celebrated, not tolerated."

- **Fourth,** you may have to end an opposite-sex friendship that is developing into an unwanted romantic relationship.

Sometimes this can happen just because you've known each other so long and it feels so "comfortable." If she wants romance and you want friendship, you have a division that will be very difficult to overcome.

Smart dating is all about knowing how to wait, whom to date, and how to relate. It means you recognize the limitations of other people and the dangers of sexual involvement or (perhaps worse) a hopelessly destructive relationship with the wrong person.

Dumb Dating

If this section were titled "dating for dummies," there would be some forms of dating that we would have to include:

Missionary Dating. "If he thinks my life is attractive, maybe it will lead him to Christ." Yeah, right. He may indeed think you're attractive, but that is likely to lead him somewhere other than Christ.

Conditional Dating. This is where you make a comment like this to someone whom you're interested in but who may not share your beliefs: "I can't go out with you unless you're a Christian." This may lead to quick conversions. The problem is, it is probably not a genuine conversion. Your comment, whether you intend it that way or not, is a setup. Your friend's motivation is more likely to be attraction and hormones than the Holy Spirit. Other conditions are many: "I'll go out with you if you . . . (fill in the blank) go to church, stop cursing, quit being violent, treat people decently, stop looking at pornography, quit drinking, etc."

Buffet Dating. On a good buffet, there are some interesting dishes that you haven't tried before. But if you're not careful, you can mix some things into your meal that make you really sick. If you "sample" people because they look really wild or exotic, you could end up with someone who can give you food poisoning.

Physical Attraction Dating. One of the most important discoveries many people make is that attractive people can sometimes be boring, dumb, obnoxious people. Many people use a lot of makeup to disguise their dysfunction. Getting to know a person you find attractive is OK, but make sure you find out what is on the inside before you turn this into a serious relationship.

Consistently Alone Dating. You need some time alone to develop a real relationship. But beware when this becomes a "hub," where your relationship is at the center and everyone else is out at the end of the spokes.

Exclusive Dating. Once you move to exclusive dating, you have put a lot of pressure on yourselves to be a couple and head toward more commitment. Other people will read it that way, too, and will treat you differently. People of the opposite sex who would like to invite you out to talk won't do so, or they will feel guilty if they do. People of the same sex will feel like you no longer have as much time for them (you won't). This is a great way to stifle most of your other friendships.

Loneliness Dating. There are times in life when we feel lonely. This is very normal, just a part of being human. We are complex beings—the most complex things on the planet—and it takes a lot to fill our huge but fragile hearts. The answer to loneliness is not necessarily to spend time with a person of the opposite sex. If the holes in our heart are caused by an absence of God, for example, no person can hope to fill them. Being with another person won't "cure" your loneliness, but it may serve to frustrate you and him, in part because you're making demands that he can't deliver on. And some people, because they are self-centered, selfish, uncaring, or just plain rotten, will actually *increase* your loneliness. There are worse things than being alone—like being with some types of people.

Fairy-tale Romance Dating. Few things are more destructive than the romance we have with "romance." Secular romance novels perpetuate the myth, and Christian publishers join in after *removing* a little sex and *adding* a little Jesus. Make no mistake, there *is* real romance. But the stuff in the novels doesn't, for the most part, exist in the real world (did you know they have *formulas* for how to write this fluff?). And it encourages our hearts to run ahead of our heads and spirits. In any relationship lived before God— which is all relationships—we want to lead with our spirits, and then with our hearts, always moderated by the experience and wisdom of our minds.

In some ways, *dumb dating* is summed up by acting as though you and the other person are more mature or committed than you really are, can handle significant time alone and really don't need others, and can grow in a safe environment without the presence and influence of other people.

The Challenges of Dating

What are the challenges of dating?

The challenges of dumb dating are immense. It will expose you to emotional, physical, and spiritual danger. It will make you an available target for nasty characters. It will make you susceptible to involvement with the first person who comes along who looks better than the crowd. It could lead to sexual participation at levels way beyond any real commitment. And it could make you cynical, as your illusions might lead you straight to disillusionment.

But there are challenges in even smart dating. You will not always have someone to do things with or to escort you to some event. Smart companies wait for first-rate people to apply rather than hiring any "warm body" that walks through the door. You should also be selective. This will make some people think you are arrogant. Others will think you're a dork or a geek.

Although the challenges of relating to people of the opposite sex have generally been the same kind through the years, they can differ in degree. One of the great challenges of life in the twenty-first century is that there is a lot more focus on the sexual (rather than the emotional) side of the relationship very early on. It is pushed at us in movies, where we often see casual or early sex presented as "normal" (even in otherwise good movies) and can now see intimate bedroom scenes played out before our eyes (is it *art* or is it *dysfunctional actors?*). And the easy availability of pornography is creating (yes, even in Christians) sexual appetites at best and sexual addiction at worst.

But premarital sexual involvement at deep levels is only one way to get entangled. In many ways, heart entanglement is much harder to sort out.

Long before you are ready to make any real commitment, you can get pulled into emotional entanglement. Even if you've tried to be smart, you have to *continue* to be smart, or you'll find yourself pulled into a relationship that is more than you bargained for. Emotional attachment can lead to mental blindness.

Going through Phases

To be really smart about this dating business, you should understand in general terms the phases that a relationship goes through.

Phase #1: Boy meets girl

This is the exciting time when you meet someone, or you get to spend time with someone you've had your eye on for a while. It feels new and fresh and romantic. You're both on your best behavior. You're eager to please. You try to say nothing that would damage this new relationship. You focus on the things that you share in common, even though real differences do exist. This other person seems, well, *ideal*. Some people get engaged during this phase. Love at first sight.

Phase #2: Boy and girl discover
they share the same interests

This is where the relationship starts to get built, and of course it's going to get built on "common ground." You find that you both like the same music and the same kind of food. Deciding what to do is easy. And they're so untypical! You can't believe that a guy really likes Jane Austen! And movies on the Lifetime channel! You can't believe she really likes action and sci-fi movies! And talking with you about cars! It's easy to be unreal, to gloss over differences, and to avoid conflict.

Engagement or marriage at this point is destined to disappoint and will often lead to disaster. What will you do when you find out she really doesn't like to watch football, or that he doesn't like to spend hours talking about your relationship? When the differences and inevitable conflict come, you feel like you were tricked. If you get committed—engaged or married—while you're still in this "whirlwind romance" phase, one thing is certain: you will have committed yourself way too soon.

Phase #3: Boy and girl discover they don't share the same interests

Now the two have known each other long enough to allow the truth to come out. Her bubbly personality, which once seemed so exciting, now embarrasses him and at times makes her seem like an airhead. His practical joking, which used to make him the life of the party, now seems to be immature and at times downright insensitive. Her quiet side now seems like dislike for other people. The differences begin to drive the couple to opposite corners. This is where a lot of relationships break off, and that's fine because here's the truth: You're not going to change this person. Not his or her basic personality. Not in this lifetime.

If these differences aren't too annoying or disturbing, you might be able to build them into a unified friendship. But you'd better take a long time and get all of these differences on the table before you get engaged or married. Saying, "We'll sort this out later" is like saying you'll study for the final after the test is over. Many too-quick marriages that happen at this phase turn cold in the end which sometimes comes quickly.

Phase #4: Boy and girl learn about unity and diversity

At this phase we start to see that differences aren't necessarily bad. They don't mean we can't have a relationship. In our humbler moments, we even see the other person's interests and strengths might complement our disinterests and weaknesses, and how differences can enhance our relationship. We learn that conflict comes in several flavors—constructive ("he really helped me see that") and destructive ("she made me feel like an idiot"). Even for this relationship to survive as a friendship, you'll need to learn how to welcome constructive conflict. You'll need to learn how to confront on real issues. If you don't confront, you will resent. And you'll need to learn how to avoid destructive conflict. People can forgive a lot easier than they can forget.

You owe it to yourself to reach this phase in your relationship just before you get engaged or married. If you don't get this right, you might still be tempted to go ahead because you've dated each other so long and have so much invested in the relationship. Great investors know when to sell their stock and take their losses. If you can't deal well with differences and conflict, my advice is to "sell."

Phase #5: Boy and girl are (maybe) still standing

If we make it through meeting, learning about similarities, learning about differences, and learning how to handle conflict well, we can begin to build something very special—at least a lifetime friendship, if not a marriage. Here is where we build on shared vision, values, and mutual trust. This is where real love starts to build. "What's so remarkable about love at first sight?" someone once asked. "It's when people have been looking at each other for years that it becomes remarkable."

Engagement or marriage in this phase makes sense. So how much time should it take to get to phase 5? What do you think?

What Is Love?

Before we go further, we ought to define *love.*

We can think of love as the opposite of hate, but in many ways love and hate are uncomfortably close together. You can see this when you watch a couple break up after they have been together for a while. They used to be crazy about each other, and now you can see the anger, especially if it was a tough breakup. When we put our hearts on the line, we're drawing water from a common source—but it can come out hot or cold.

Love is perhaps better described as the opposite of indifference. Love is the "hot" that moves us away from the "lukewarm." God makes it clear that you are closer to Him when your feelings are running deep—either hot or cold—than when they are just existing at room temperature: "I wish that you were cold or hot. So, because you are lukewarm, and neither hot nor cold, I am going to vomit you out of My mouth" (Revelation 3:15b–16). So love is the force that drives us away from being bored, uninterested, and indifferent—either about God or about another person.

Real love starts with obedience and self-control (see 1 Peter 1:22). We must be sincere about God before we can be sincere about another person. And if love is going to reach into and flow out of our core, we must not just be involved with "believers," but with those believers who are wise, sincere, and deep. We will be the same as we are now in five years except for the decisions we make, the things we read and study, and the people we spend time with.

Real love is not self-seeking (see 1 Corinthians 13:5). Paul said about his friend Timothy, "I have no one else like him, who takes a genuine interest in your welfare" (Philippians 2:20 NIV). Many people have the words, but few will have a genuine interest in you, except maybe to possess you. A possessiveness born out of loneliness, desperation, and unresolved issues isn't love at all, but a destructive, devouring dependency. Dependency, which you hear touted in so many popular songs as "love" ("I can't make it without you, baby") is parasitical and is really *anti-love*. And we can't start being loving and generous just because we're "in love." If we're selfish with everyone but a "romantic" partner, we will be selfish there, too, when the glow wears off. We're told to give, and *then* we will receive (see Acts 20:35).

Real love is patient (see 1 Corinthians 13:4). Could you wait five years and still want to marry the same person? If not, why not? Expecting another to meet our needs puts a heavy burden on the relationship. Marriage isn't the answer to our problems, but it may compound and add to existing problems (see 1 Corinthians 7:28b). And children can compound the grief even more. Real love can always wait.

The best love isn't married love; it's agape love, soul-to-soul love, *wherever* we find it (see 1 Corinthians 13:13). It is in every great friendship. And it should be in marriage, but often it is not. It can be very difficult to find the real deal. Parents need to pray for their children's future *discernment*, not only for their children's future spouses.

What role does God's love for us play in our understanding of human love? How should we develop ourselves to be loving people, who discern other loving people with whom we can relate on an intimate basis?

Being Holy and Pure

How do you learn to relate to the opposite sex, with all of the excitement that brings, and still remain holy and pure? Is it possible? (We'll talk about this fully in chap. 12 on sex—no, don't flip over there just yet!)

You can't pull it off no matter how hard you try. The reason is that you have a sinful nature. It's like a guerrilla warrior who lives inside of you. It has its own cravings and desires. You might want to serve God and love that other person with holiness, but this guerrilla has its own agenda. It listens to the corrupt world system that surrounds all of us. It listens to the Enemy.

And it doesn't go away when you become a Christian. It can't be eliminated and it won't be transformed (Romans 7:15–25; 8:6–7, 12–14). In fact—and let's face it, this is a hard, sad truth—"The old sinful nature loves to do evil, which is just opposite from what the Holy Spirit wants. And the Spirit gives us desires that are opposite from what the sinful nature desires. These two forces are constantly fighting each other, *and your choices are never free from this conflict*" (Galatians 5:17 NLT, emphasis added). What does this mean? No matter how much you love this other person, no matter how decent you are trying to be, your own sinful nature is lurking in the shadows and hoping to bring you down into the dirt. Don't trust it. Be aware of when it is driving you to hurt or use this other person for your own benefit.

This means that only dependence on the power of the indwelling Holy Spirit can cause you to maintain purity.

Sex isn't a time bomb set to blow up our lives. It is fun and enjoyable and pleasurable. And sex is quite down to earth. Sex, in spite of the consistent teaching of the church since Augustine more than fifteen hundred years ago, is not dirty. But by talking about it as though it's dirty and acting like it's dirty, we can end up with a self-fulfilling reality that for us, it *is* dirty. Now, the Enemy knows how to use to his own ends the truth that sex is fun and down to earth and that most of us are trained to think it's dirty. Treating sex as either "sacred" or "dirty" is not dealing in reality, and it is unlikely to help us one way or the other.

The only way to succeed is to beat the temptation to misuse sex. The way to be holy is to run to the Lord every day, to "crucify" the sinful nature daily, to go to Him a thousand times in a day if the attacks come that often. You have God's grace, which instructs us "to deny godlessness and worldly lusts" (Titus 2:12).

The bottom line is that you shouldn't be saving yourself only for marriage. You should also be saving yourself for a great, God-centered marriage. We don't avoid immorality only for the sake of our future spouse. We avoid immorality to honor God.

And maybe, just maybe, saving yourself for yourself.

Final Thought

You can't live an effective life as a hermit: "One who isolates himself pursues [selfish] desires; he rebels against all sound judgment" (Proverbs 18:1). This is the best time of your life to get out and experience the wonder that is other human beings, and the wonder with a twist that is human beings of the opposite sex.

But you need to do it smart. So kiss dumb dating good-bye.

And develop the most outstanding friendships of anyone on the planet.

Discussion Questions

On Your Own

- *Ask Your Parents:* Can you tell me about any dumb dating that you did? What did you learn? What did you do when you dated that seems smart now as you look back?

- *Ask Your Youth Pastor or Pastor:* What biblical principles do you think apply to dating?

Together

- *Ask Each Other:* What do you think "dating" is? (Discuss the "Ten Keys to Building Great Friendships.") How well have we done in developing a great friendship? What are the biggest challenges you've faced in dating me or others?

Facing the Sobering Realities about Relationships and Marriage

Part 2

In olden times sacrifices were made at the altar,
A custom that is still continued.
Helen Rowland

before you tie the knot, make sure the rope isn't around your neck

chapter 5

You only have one life and so many years to live.

The impact of fuzzy or false thinking in this important area of serious relationships will be felt in every corner of your life and for all of your days. The victory, the success, is there—*if you live in wisdom*. But there is also a sober warning: before you tie the knot, make sure the rope isn't around your neck.

You know what the problem is? You don't have to come up with a bad strategy to end up in a bad relationship. All you have to do is avoid thinking about where your current thoughts and feelings are taking you. Just not thinking clearly and biblically about these issues can lead you into some real problems.

Thus grief still treads upon the heels of pleasure,
Marry'd in haste, we may repent at leisure.
William Congreve

"I'm too young to worry about this stuff," you or your friend might be saying. You know what? If you're old enough to spend time alone with others, if you're old enough to enjoy their company, if you're old enough to get hurt deeply by them—in other words, if you're old enough to get emotionally involved—then you're *not* too young to worry about this stuff. In fact, you're too young *not* to be worried about this stuff. Now is the very time when too many people walk through a beautiful green field and step in a cow pie.

If you're smart enough to be reading this book, you're smart enough to keep your head *above* the sand rather than sticking it *into* the sand.

The Real Truth about Marriage

Marriage.

A wonderful, glorious, thrilling word. But it can also be a disillusioning, chilling word. "Marriage is heaven and hell," an old German proverb reminds us. The potential rewards of marriage are fabulous, but the risks are just as gigantic. You can find the love of a lifetime and win big—or you can slide into a trap (even with a decent person!) and end up making a big mistake. Poor decisions about things like your education and career are small compared to poor decisions here.

Marriage isn't like taking a course that looks interesting in school. You find out early on that it's really *not* that interesting, and you're getting a C or D as well. So you withdraw before the deadline to keep it from showing up on your school records. Now, part of these two things (a poor marriage or a course) is the same—you *can* find out early on in a marriage that you're getting a C or D (or F). But you can't withdraw before the deadline because it is a real deadline—the "till death do us part" kind.

Marriage can be like playing the lottery, with its offer of instant and bountiful rewards. From the outside, marriage can look like it will satisfy most of our emotional needs.

What are our wants? We want marriage to make us totally happy, and we really don't want marriage to change us. We want to be loved just as we are, with unconditional love. We want marriage to cure our loneliness and fix our emotional wounds. We want to seal up a relationship that we can count on, that won't go away. We want marriage to make us a more complete person. We want it to open up possibilities that we couldn't otherwise have. We want a storybook romance, just like all the Christian romance novels tell us about. And we want God to keep us out of a bad marriage.

Not likely.

Our unrealistic expectations of marriage can make it unable to deliver them. Only when we back off of our list of wants and understand what marriage really is, can we possibly hope to find any of the good results that we want. Getting a lot out of marriage starts with understanding the real truth about marriage. Following are some truths that you won't hear in romance novels or most churches.

Real Truth #1: While marriage can lead to great happiness, the truth is that marriage is *not* necessarily designed to make you happy. In fact, marriage will probably make you unhappy on a frequent basis, even if it's a good marriage. It will probably make you deeply unhappy even if it's a *great* marriage, in part because great marriages work overtime to rub off your rough edges. Happiness will come only if we persist through the hard learning, live our lives well, and then receive happiness as the by-product of our labor.

Real Truth #2: Marriage *is* designed to change you. It won't leave you just as you are, with all of the self-centeredness and pettiness that it is so easy for human beings to exhibit. A lot of people say going in that they hope marriage will make them better people, but most just don't want any *pain* on the journey to being better. They want marriage to make them better persons by the other person *pretending* that they are better people, and by telling them how wonderful and perfect they are. Real change is painful. In a marriage relationship, you're likely to face some pain that always accompanies constructive change.

Real Truth #3: Marriage is a *very* conditional relationship. We all *like* this *unconditional love* stuff. As good as this concept sounds, unfortunately, it is not very real in practice. We all know that it's hard to love people when they treat us harshly. The Bible is full of references to *unfailing* love, but love is a very conditional thing. If you treat her like dirt, she won't be able to love you. If you want him to love you, you'd better respect him.

God Himself has conditional love. If you don't love Him, if you don't repent and confess and receive His free gift of salvation sometime before you die, you have not met the conditions and you will suffer the consequences eternally. Just know that God has given His all to have a loving, unfailing, eternal relationship with you, so you can live an eternal life with Him.

Real Truth #4: Being married will not cure your loneliness or heal your lonely "inner child," but it could make these things worse. The more you demand time and attention from your spouse, the less likely she will probably be to give it (at least after she figures out she can never give enough to satisfy you). And if you are really insecure or emotionally damaged, you will probably choose someone who will make you feel even more insecure, emotionally damaged, and lonelier than you do now. Marriage won't cure anything, because it's a relationship and not a prescription.

I've known many young men, for example, who believed that getting married would solve a lust problem or an addiction. It's more likely that the moon is made of green cheese.

But marriage between two emotionally healthy people offers a lifetime of mutual sharing and togetherness. There are very few things that are quite so liberating and emotionally rewarding as two people who give themselves to each other in a marriage relationship.

Real Truth #5: Marriage won't guarantee your security. It won't guarantee that you have this other person securely in your grasp forever. Vows and licenses won't make any difference if his character is flawed and he doesn't really commit. Your only security is in God and the wisdom, insight, power, and strength He will give you if you ask.

Tabitha was convinced that Jeff was going to stop flirting with other girls after he bought her a ring on Valentine's Day. She was shocked when he spent an entire dinner hitting on the waitress. Tabitha hadn't learned that rings don't change people.

Real Truth #6: It's true that marriage will make you a more complete, rounded, and effective person, but you probably won't enjoy the process. You will think that your way is best and that your partner is defective for seeing or doing things differently. You won't even *believe* some of the things she will push you to do. If you survive the process you will be a better person, but the process will not be pleasant. Growth always involves some pain.

Real Truth #7: Marriage has its compensations and rewards, but it also carries a price. At times, you will miss your freedom and what my daughter Laura calls "the shimmering glow of possibility just around the corner." You will miss the exciting sense that you could meet someone breathtaking or do something dazzling at any time. You won't be able to go everywhere you want, when you want, with whom you want. Life will likely settle into a routine, some of which will not be very interesting.

Real Truth #8: The only storybook romances are in storybooks. Marriage is more about what you build together than about what you were on your wedding day or honeymoon. Matches made by God Himself—Adam and Eve, Isaac and Rebekah—produced marriages that led to problems. In other words, even if God puts you in the path of a great person made just for you, your choices can still mess it up if you don't build with good materials on a good foundation. You will have to commit yourself to building something valuable with a very difficult person (which we all are) to whom you have joined your life.

Real Truth #9: For the marriage to work, you will have to ignore a lot. There will be the daily frustrations, where you will be bouncing off each other in all of the activities that make up daily life, an experience totally different than dating. Children will bring issues—many more than you can imagine—that bring sacrifices as well as rewards. I have watched the excitement and spontaneity go out of hundreds of marriages in the face of little children, dirty diapers, and dealing with their full-time demands. A wife will go through some reevaluations and transitions, in her thirties and then again later. A husband will go through several transitions and probably at least one major midlife crisis (reevaluation) in his forties. All of these adjustments take love and patience on the part of both husband and wife.

Real Truth #10: God will not keep you out of a bad marriage. *No one* will keep you out of a bad marriage in a free country. The decision to get into a marriage is yours. If you want to get into a bad marriage—if you want to ignore God's guidance, if you don't listen to sound advice, if you don't believe that the things in this book are real—then you can do so. But it won't be God's fault. You'll see the cause staring back at you in the mirror.

On this last point, we should talk for a minute about God's will. Many young people wrestle over what "God's will" means, and this is a good thing to do. But God never once in the Bible tells you His "will" about a possible marriage partner. If you look up the Scriptures on "God's will," you will see that He has all sorts of guidance about this. For example:

- It is God's will **"that everyone who sees the Son and believes in Him may have eternal life"** (John 6:40a; see also Galatians 1:4). In other words, it's His will that you first get bonded to Him, not to any particular person.
- **"Rejoice always! Pray constantly. Give thanks in everything,** *for this is God's will for you in Christ Jesus"* (1 Thessalonians 5:16–18; emphasis added). Can you be joyful even when you don't have a date? Can you pray continually, even when you're spending time with her? Can

you give thanks, even after he dumped you and it hurts so bad? If not, there's one thing we know for sure from this verse: *You aren't in the will of God.*

- **"For it is God's will that you, by doing good, silence the ignorance of foolish people"** (1 Peter 2:15). A lot of dating stirs up the talk of foolish people more than it silences it.

- **"For it is better to suffer for doing good, if that should be God's will, than for doing evil"** (1 Peter 3:17). Relationships offer lots of chances to suffer. The question is, Are you going to suffer for being a person of honor and integrity, or for getting involved in stupidity and sin?

- **Jesus prayed, "Yet not as I will, but as You will"** (Matthew 26:39). It's really important to separate our will from God's. Are you willing to do that? Are you willing to give up a person because he isn't in God's will for you—even if he makes your heart skip a beat?

- **"God wants you to be holy, so you should keep clear of all sexual sin. Then each of you will control your body and live in holiness and honor—not in lustful passion as the pagans do, in their ignorance of God and his ways. Never cheat a Christian brother in this matter by taking his wife, for the Lord avenges all such sins"** (1 Thessalonians 4:3–6 NLT). God is more concerned with your behavior with all others than He is about you finding Mr. Right or Miss Right. But He certainly wants you to make the right choice in the important matters of marriage.

It is God's will that you relate to Him and all others well, but it is never said in the Bible that it is His will that you marry Bill rather than Marc, Jessica rather than Kayla. You might be able to make a good marriage or a bad marriage with either one. God will never "will" anyone into your life. You are free to marry anyone who will accept your proposal. There is no magical, step-by-step formula that will guarantee success. And you are not a pre-programmed, puppet-on-a-string dancing at the "will" of God.

So what are we saying about marriage? Marriage won't make you happy or successful or spiritual or anything else. It will open up certain possibilities and close out others, which may make you unhappy but is unlikely to do the reverse. However, a Christ-centered marriage can be greatly used by God to enhance your life and to help you grow and mature.

Your happiness, success, and spirituality must be qualities of your own soul and your own relationship with God. No one can put in what you've left out.

Some Painful Realities

Statistics have consistently shown over recent decades that about one in every two marriages ends in divorce or separation. The current numbers are 50 percent within twenty years of marriage. But the number jumps to 67 percent for young women who are married before age eighteen and 56 percent for young women who are married when they are between eighteen and nineteen. When we get to women twenty to twenty-four years old, the number drops to 41 percent.[1] Here are some painful realities these statistics make clear:

Reality #1: Marriage is a risky business, with a 50-50 chance of success and failure even if you wait. Christians aren't immune from this. Many people who thought they would never get divorced—many who once *condemned* divorce—end up getting one when the ugliness is more than they think they can bear. You might be thinking, "I'll be in the stick-it-out 50 percent." The problem is, That's what *everyone* thinks going in. And even if you would never divorce, you can't control the other person. Vows and covenants offer only the illusion of security.

Reality #2: In view of the risk of disaster and divorce, marriage for teenagers and very young people is a bad plan. The younger you are when you marry, the smaller the opportunity you've had to learn who you are, what other people are really like, and what it takes to make a good thing out of a relationship. You might think you are mature enough as a very young person to make the decision to get engaged or married. The devil is dancing at the thought.

Reality #3: Even many marriages that stay together lose their glow over time. According to one study of people during their first ten years of marriage, couples say that the quality of the relationship starts to go down soon after the honeymoon and *continues* going down for the first four years. Then it levels off for a few years before resuming the decline in years eight, nine, and ten. The study showed that children don't help this situation. In fact, the presence of children adds a lot of stress and can actually speed up the decline.[2] "The facts of life are very grinding, so the reality of marriage is grinding," says Natalie Low, a clinical psychologist and instructor at Harvard.[3]

In a recent poll in Britain, one in four married couples admitted that they regret getting married. A total of 44 percent of women and 39 percent of men said they had a secret they would never tell their spouse. And to show how much the "excitement" of marriage can decline, middle-aged couples were five times more likely to fantasize about having a dog than about having sex![4]

Reality #4: With the high rates and acceptability of divorce, things have gotten so scary that many people have decided just to live together in sort of a "semimarriage." This looks to some like a middle ground between singleness and marriage. But the question is whether this is "middle ground" or "no-man's-land." According to the National Marriage Project at Rutgers University, *couples who live together without getting married are more likely to face many domestic problems—including divorce if they ever do get married.* "People like to call it a trial marriage," says Michael McManus of Marriage Savers. "It would be a better idea to call it a trial divorce."[5]

In addition to the moral issues, the essential problem is adding the friction of daily life to the low-commitment relationship. In attempting to have the best of both worlds, singleness and marriage, we can end up with little of the joy of either. Unfortunately, living together gives you all of the problems and annoyances of being married, but without the dedication.

Reality #5: Even more extreme, others are talking about "starter" marriages. A starter marriage is "a union between those in their twenties and thirties who marry for five years or less and divorce without having kids . . . When the time comes to start a family, they take a look at their marriage; if it doesn't seem right, they just end it."[6] This ignores the fact, of course, that people who marry have *already* started a family. And how many of us want to be somebody's experiment?

Here's some even more important news: Although practice may make perfect in some areas of life, it doesn't work very well with marriage. According to the study discussed at the beginning of this section, the divorce rate after ten years for those who are remarried is 39 percent, significantly higher than the 33 percent of first marriages that end in divorce after ten years.[7] And guess what? Even on remarriage, the divorce rate is higher the younger you are when you remarry.

What does this mean for you? If you're thinking, "This person could be a possible spouse," the next thought you have should be a question: "Am I possibly out of my mind?" If you're even slightly uncomfortable with this person before you tie any emotional knots, you have to remember this may just be the tip of a monstrous iceberg.

If you think wisely and choose well, these statistics won't become *your* reality.

Making It Harder to Hang Yourself

People talk a lot today about making it harder to get divorced, but that's working at the wrong end of relational disease. We should be making it harder to get *married*—but not with rules and regulations, approvals and vetoes, or some sort of "weeding out" program like Navy Seals training.

Instead, we should make it harder by learning how to think clearly and biblically about the three crucial components of successful marriage decisions.

Component #1: Yourself. If we haven't evaluated who we are and where we are on the maturity scale, we have almost no chance of making a good marriage decision. This comes before all else. Are we becoming a high-quality person who invests in other people? Are we taking steps to becoming a better person, whether or not we end up getting married? Are we aware of the "holes" in our own hearts? If not, we will be unable to see clearly, to separate the wheat from the chaff, to pick out the wolves in sheep's clothing. Even if we stumble across a terrific person, if we haven't made it through this first component we are a disaster waiting to be inflicted on a marriage partner.

Component #2: The Other Person. If we're thinking clearly about ourselves, we're ready to begin thinking clearly about other people. Now we can see past the facades, the superficial compatibility, the emotional entanglements that seem so much like a Hollywood movie. We can evaluate who they are, their strengths and weaknesses, and where they are on the maturity scale. Are we sure we aren't falling into one of the problems that we should never marry? Is this person driven by a desire to invest in others, or a leechlike need to drain the life from those around him or her? Rare treasures are hard to find.

Component #3: The "Match." Even if we and the other person are on solid footing, the case is not closed. Two decent, strong people can still make an ugly marriage. We can love without marrying, and we can't marry everyone we love: "He gave his sons just one piece of advice," said Cleveland Amory; "never confuse 'I love you' with 'I want to marry you.'" Do we know the right reasons to get married? Have we done an honest assessment of key things we *must* be sure of if we want to win it all? Do we really know the secrets of picking out *the one* from the "many"? Architectural masterpieces begin with craftsmanship in *design.* Happy, rewarding marriages, like exquisite buildings, do not happen by chance.

Although the third area above might seem like a long way in the future for you, you can use this material as a grid that you can relate to now—and know how to apply later.

Don't wait for your church, your parents, or the government to make up some rules that will keep you out of a disastrous relationship. They may be able to offer some valuable counsel. But only you, with God's help, can make the right choice.

The Rope around Your Neck

Do you realize that you can put the rope around your own neck? There are a number of ways to tie the knot around your neck. They will leave you saying, "What on earth happened?" The following are a few of the biggest ones.

Looking for a Spouse

I've heard many young women talk about going to college for their "MRS" degree (which is often more of a BS degree). Bad plan. Unbiblical plan. God says, "Are you unmarried? *Do not look for a wife*" (1 Corinthians 7:27b NIV; emphasis added). This one piece of advice from God, if it were followed, would cut out a huge percentage of the nonsense that goes on between the sexes. Did you know that many "helps" can't really help you? How should you react if you see a book titled *How to Know If Someone Is Worth Pursuing in Two Dates or Less*? Even if someone were worth pursuing, we've got no business doing it. And marriage is a *relationship*, not a position or status to be sought with some mysterious person "out there."

We're not supposed to be on some kind of FBI investigation, a search for the *one most wanted*, using two dates as a checklist to eliminate suspects. Instead of looking for a spouse, our time would be better spent looking at both troubled and happy marriages and taking notes.

Getting Emotionally Committed

Jessica and Matt have gone out a few times. Before either of them realize it, all of their friends start thinking of them as a couple. Now, in addition to their own emotions and needs, they've got peer pressure and expectations working against them. Every time a friend says something that deals with them as a couple, that idea will get more cemented in everyone's mind. But here's the bottom line: None of Jessica's or Matt's friends will have to live with a bad marriage, if that's what they're heading for. Long after most of those friends are distant memories, Jessica and Matt will still be living out the pressure and comments of those old, ghostly voices.

Any decent person (and, scary to say, many indecent people) can come along and meet our current emotional needs. We should thank them. We should return the favor, if we can do so appropriately. But we shouldn't think that this will translate into them meeting any of our emotional needs even six months from now. If Jessica and Matt have the good sense that God gave them, they will enjoy their emotions without letting them run wild. They will have Spirit-*controlled*, self-*controlled* passion. If you don't think that's possible, you're not ready to be real with anyone of the opposite sex.

Thinking No One Else Will Come Along

One of the great lies of the Enemy is that, as Elvis once sang, it's "Now or Never." This person may be as good as it gets. But we've got to get the order right. We don't have to keep waiting if we're sure we've found *the one*. But we don't stop waiting if we have the slightest doubt.

Juries might convict if the evidence is beyond a "reasonable doubt," but you had better go beyond even the *unreasonable* doubt. There are several hundred million people of the opposite sex who are roughly your age. It's a large pool. Keep swimming until you have no doubt.

Rebounding

Sarah had just finished breaking up with Josh after two years, and she was heartsick. She hadn't been alone for a long time. She didn't have anyone to do things with, and all of her friends had serious boyfriends. She always felt weird going along by herself, and she hated having people feel sorry for her. Then it happened! Magic! Brett was a dream—even better than Josh. Sarah could tell him anything. She was hooked. The breakup with Josh still hurt when she allowed herself to think about it, but being with Brett made it all seem so long ago.

Brett may make better medicine for a broken heart in the short run than a relationship for a maturing Sarah in the long run. The problem is that even if she senses that Brett isn't the one for her, it will be very hard to let go of the guy who *rescued* her. And she will really resist letting a *second* relationship get away. She can end up hooked and miss the best because she let her life be controlled by a broken heart.

Your friends might encourage you to get out and meet some new people after you've lost a relationship. But if you're wise you'll take it slow and allow yourself time to recover. Plenty of time. This is the time for Sarah to get in touch with herself and God, not with a male heart-saver.

Sharing Unequally

Over the long run, great relationships are born from a balance of talking and sharing our inner thoughts. There are a lot of speakers and writers who talk jokingly about women saying three to five times more words a day than men. Maybe this is true, *but you'd better make sure it isn't true in your relationship.* There is a trend toward less openness: "Beginning in the teens and '20s of [the last] century, both sexes became less committed to the kind of openness and self-expression that earlier generations had strived for."[8]

How can you know this other person, if you're talking 70 or 80 or 90 percent of the time? What is he leaving out? Why is he holding back? Maybe the same things he will be leaving out and holding back for the rest of your life.

Spending More Time Shopping for a Car than Protecting Your Future

Buying a car is great fun, and we want to make sure we get just the right one. Most people spend more time finding and buying a car than they do on thinking seriously about the second most important relationship of their lives. (The most important is our relationship with God.)

If you make a wrong decision about a car, you can dump it and try again. You can't be too careful when buying a car. You can easily get a lemon, or pay too much. Compare that to inviting someone into your life to be a part of every decision for the rest of your life. Makes you stop and think. Or at least it should.

Forgetting How Long the Results Will Last

If you have a new bicycle or a new car, right now it looks great. But the end of these beautiful things, in ten or twenty years or before, will be rust. But after twenty years of a rusty and decaying marriage, you might still have thirty or forty years to go. That's a long time to be unhappy and frustrated.

When Jesus explained the permanency of marriage to His followers, you know what their response was? "If the relationship of a man with his wife is like this, it's better not to marry" (Matthew 19:10). He wasn't saying that marriage was bad. He was just saying that it is a permanent relationship.

Getting Pregnant

You probably already have the power to make a baby. But you also have the power to do it too soon. You can hurt your life and two other lives—the person making the baby with you, and the baby herself. Having to get married because of a pregnancy is a lousy basis for a marriage. If you do get married, you have a new human being who may live in a dysfunctional family. And as a Christian—as a *human being*—you have no right to abort that baby, to eliminate the so-called "mistake" that is actually a supernatural being made in the image of God. God says that you can't put your "sons and daughters in the fire" (Jeremiah 7:31).[9]

God will certainly forgive you for getting ahead of yourself and having a baby. But you should be aware that the consequences could go on for the rest of your life.

Now for some good news.

If there is a rope there to hang us, there is also a rope from heaven to pull us out of danger. But we have to reach out for that lifeline. Uncomfortable, slightly out-of-whack things during the time before a marriage—even during wedding planning—could be just the warning shot before the battle that will go on and on. Reach for the lifeline, now and every day. Let God pull you out of self-deception into a great life based on truth.

Guarantees, Defenses, and Loopholes

If you go to buy a new sound system or computer in an electronics store, the sales clerk will probably talk with you about a warranty. When you buy something or have work done on your car, you want some sort of guarantee that the product or the repair will really *work*. In most cases, you'd be crazy not to get a warranty, probably even an extended warranty.

It would be nice if we could get a marriage warranty—a guarantee that things will work out well. The first company that can offer such a guarantee will rake in the profits. But no one can offer a marriage guarantee, because it doesn't exist. The most you can hope to do is eliminate as many of the questions and doubts and pitfalls as you can before you get too serious.

So what are some of the things people use as marriage guarantees?

The Engagement Defense

Some people use the engagement defense. They say, "We're engaged, but we're not going to get married until next year." They can believe that they have one last chance to back out. We really *do* have a chance to back out during the engagement, but it is very hard to take this opportunity when the relationship has gone this far.

An engagement is a statement to the world that we are heading toward *marriage*. We've set a goal for everyone to see. They will expect us to achieve the goal. We can work very hard at this point to avoid talking about problems or real issues, because they seem out of place because we're in love. Instead, we'll be tempted to put a "good face" on everything. Engagement is usually thought of as *marriage-preparation* time rather than *work-on-the-relationship-and-make-sure-we're-ready-for-marriage* time.

The engagement process takes on a life of its own, with planning and decisions and picking out flowers and dresses and tuxes and dishes. We'll introduce the other person with a special name, and it will be *my fiancé* rather than *my possible life disaster*. And if we get engaged before phase 5—the phase in which boy and girl are still standing—we're likely in a fairy-tale dream that we don't want to end.

Engagement is, in practice, the same as tying the knot. Engagement is not your marriage defense. Your *brain* is your defense.

The Premarital Counseling Defense

Maybe your church has a premarital program for engaged couples. Maybe it's even an unusual one that includes a number of sessions over a number of months. Doesn't this offer a measure of safety? No way. If you're relying on these to keep you out of catastrophe, you're probably a dead duck. Most of these programs *assume* you are going to get married. Premarital counseling seldom if ever causes an engagement to end. That's not one of its purposes (although it should be).

What churches need are premarital programs for people who *aren't* engaged or thinking about marriage. No-baloney sessions in youth groups will beat after-the-fact, postengagement programs because people can still hear at least a little, and because youth pastors are often more willing to tell it like it is than busy pastors who are planning a wedding. (If your youth pastor isn't like this, you might ask him to start telling it like it is. Or you might find a youth group or church where you can hear the truth.)

The Relationship Tools Defense

There is a philosophy that if a couple understands each other's likes and dislikes, and can agree on how they *think* a marriage should work, then their relationship will be a happy one. It thinks of marriage excellence primarily as a functional issue. Give people the right tools, and they can get the job done. It's sort of a *scientific management* approach to the problem.

Essentially, this line of attack says that any two decent people could marry and make it work, as long as they develop their *compatibility* and learn to use some effective relational techniques (like communication and conflict resolution). The appropriateness of the "match," and even of marriage itself at that time, are often not seriously considered.

Is marriage for everyone? No. Will good relational skills save a bad match? No. You can't dig up gold with a good shovel *if there isn't any gold*. Most marriage preparation books leave out the most critical questions, some of the great questions of a lifetime: Should you get married at all? Are you becoming a person worth marrying? Is this person, no matter how high quality she seems, becoming a person worth marrying? If so, is this person the best choice for me? The rest of this book is designed to help you answer these crucial questions.

So here's the scoop: Relational tools won't help much if you don't get the big questions answered correctly. They can make a good marriage better. They can help save a marriage from total disaster. But they can't save a marriage from mediocrity.

Conclusion

The battle to save marriages has to be won before the weddings occur—*long* before the weddings occur. Because weddings result from our thinking, actions, and decisions, it's essential that we know how to think and act and decide biblically *before* we find ourselves in emotionally charged relationships that cannot easily be broken off.

Marriages based on erroneous and unbiblical thinking about life and love will rarely flourish through the passage of time and the storms of life. You need to understand yourself and other people as individuals first, and then you need to understand your relationship. And you need to be aware of all of this *before*—not after—you take the important step.

So if you're reading this the night before your wedding and have any doubts, call it off. At least put it off—delay it until your spirit and mind are clear. Even if you're at the *altar* and have doubts, stop the music and turn it into an open house or a party for your friends and family. Embarrassment is a lot better than tragedy.

And one last thought: Before you tie the knot, make sure the rope isn't around your neck.

Discussion Questions

On Your Own

- *Ask Your Parents:* How has marriage changed you (good and bad)? How has marriage affected your feelings of loneliness? What possibilities did getting married and having children eliminate from your life? (That one should make them squirm!) How did getting married affect your feelings of romance? What do you really think of my friend?

- *Ask Your Youth Pastor or Pastor:* What percentage of marriages do you think is really happy? Why? What is the difference between unconditional love and unfailing love? What is the number-one tip you could give to help me stay out of a bad marriage?

Together

- *Ask Each Other:* Are we moving too fast? Are we letting other people treat us as a couple or pressure us in any way? How do you think marriage will change you? How do you think it will change me? How do you think we would react to these changes? Are you comfortable with our level of emotional involvement and commitment?
- *Ask Your Youth Pastor or Pastor:* Do you see anything in our relationship that you also have seen in any troubled marriages? What percentage of marriages do you think is really happy? Why? What three main things will each of us have to ignore about the other if we get more serious? What is the number-one tip you could give us to help us avoid getting into a bad marriage?

Such people [those who marry] will have trouble in this life, and I am trying to spare you.
1 Corinthians 7:28b

twelve lousy reasons for getting married

chapter 6

A woman waiting for a plane in a busy airport bought a package of cookies and a newspaper. After scouting around, she sat down at a small table in a busy corridor.

A few minutes later, she heard a crackling of paper. She looked around her newspaper and was shocked to see that a man had sat down uninvited, just a few feet away. Worse, he had opened the package of cookies, taken a cookie, and put it in his mouth! She quickly went back behind her newspaper.

Who is this man? she asked herself. *What on earth does he think he's doing?* Then she heard more noise, and peeked around her paper to see him taking another cookie.

Feeling a sudden surge of anger, she snatched a cookie from the package on the table and defiantly took a bite. Undaunted, the man took another cookie from the package—and then another! And the jerk was smiling! She wanted to say something but responded instead by

Marriage is the only evil that men pray for.
Greek proverb

eating another one herself, as fast as she could—glaring at him all the while.

Finally, only one cookie was left in the package. This arrogant man took the cookie and, while she watched in a stunned swirl of emotions, broke it in two. He shoved half of the cookie toward her, and then put the other half in his mouth as he rose to leave. She was so angry that she crushed her half of the cookie in her hand. She sat there shaking, so angry she couldn't move.

Finally, she looked down at her watch and saw that it was past time to go to her gate. In addition to everything else, this fool had made her late. She jumped up, grabbed her bags, and dashed to the check-in line. She opened her purse to get her ticket and ID—and found there her unopened package of cookies.

Making Assumptions

Making assumptions is a dangerous practice.

All of us have made assumptions about life, ourselves, and other people that we later realized—often to our horror—were wrong. The consequences can be as minor as a few moments of embarrassment, like our friend with the cookies. But if we base important life decisions on these "irreverent and silly myths" (1 Timothy 4:7), the horror can last for the rest of our lives.

You know what causes good decision-making to be even more challenging? Much of what influences our decisions comes from an undercurrent of ideas and needs that is often invisible to our conscious minds. These hidden motivators or influences can push us into bad decisions that we later regret. Without reflection, we may not even know why we chose those things in the first place.

Over and over again I have asked serious and sincere people to rate all of the marriages they have ever known on a scale of "poor–fair–average–very good–excellent." At first some will put 25 percent or more in the top two categories. But if they are pressed to be honest and evaluate only the marriages they know well, they seldom rate more than 5 to 10 percent of those marriages in the combined "very good" and "excellent" categories.

The purpose of this chapter is to help you (and maybe a friend or two) think about some of the bad reasons people use as a basis for marriage. Unfortunately, this list is not a complete list. My hope is that you will use this as a checklist and as a prompter of additional thought.

There are some seriously flawed reasons that drive many marriage decisions. Part of good thinking is to make sure we aren't getting a distorted picture of other people by looking at them through a broken glass.

So let's take a close look at the twelve lousy reasons to get married.

Reason #1: You Think You Are "Called" to Marriage

Kate was a young woman who had attended the same church as Sean for several years. Sean was a widower twenty years her senior with five children, while Kate was just out of high school. One day Kate went to Sean and told him that God had "revealed" to her that she was to marry him. He was shocked at this suggestion because he had no intention of marrying again.

However, Kate's boldness and claim of "calling" were so strong that Sean began to consider the possibility. They eventually did marry, which brought grief to both of them as well as the children. They disliked almost everything about each other, and she was a harsh and unfocused mother. Her claim of "calling" influenced Sean to do something that he might otherwise have realized was foolish. It led her into a demoralizing relationship that wasted her youth.

Over the years, I have heard many people say in one form or another that they were "called" to marriage. The problem is that we can *sanitize* our desires by claiming a "calling."

This can end up as a self-determining course, as it did with Shannon, a young woman who claimed to have a clear and special leading from the Lord. She said God "told" her that she would be married within a year, although she didn't know to whom. Sure enough, she was a bride within a year. Shannon said her original direction was a "prophecy"—but it was more on the order of the "self-fulfilling" kind. The marriage turned out to be suffocating and ended in divorce.

The truth is that God "calls" us to follow *Him* (Matthew 6:33; Ephesians 4:1). He specifically says, "Are you unmarried? *Do not look for a wife*" (1 Corinthians 7:27b; emphasis added). In following him, we will be led into relationships with people, but not necessarily into a specific *form* of relationship (like marriage).

Marriage isn't a calling. It's a *relationship.* We must get away from the notion that everyone is supposed to get married and that people should begin their search for a prospective spouse as young adults.

The idea of marriage as a calling is ridiculous. Unfortunately, if you use it as a reason to marry, it can be very deadly.

Reason #2: You Are Lonely or Needy

Terrell was in his early twenties, and he lived alone in a nice apartment complex. He attended some events sponsored by several people who lived in his building, but these events were attended mostly by couples (married and otherwise). He usually came away feeling even lonelier than before.

Terrell began attending his church's singles ministry for people ages eighteen to thirty. To his surprise and delight he found two young women, both nineteen, who seemed to like him. Tamika was introverted and struck him as even lonelier than he was. Sheila, on the other hand, always tried to sit near him and was desperate for his attention. Terrell divided his time between them, at both the church meetings and in one-on-one dates.

Although Terrell liked Tamika more in many ways, after two years he finally married Sheila. He told himself, "She really needs me, and it feels good to be needed." Their marriage started out as a tug of war, with Terrell wanting relaxed companionship that Sheila couldn't give, and Sheila wanting him to fix things in her life that he couldn't make better. This collision of loneliness and neediness ended up with two people even emptier than before. Terrell felt used and drained, and Sheila felt a sense of betrayal.

So what if Terrell had married Tamika, the lonely person, instead? Is loneliness a sound basis for a healthy marriage? The answer is "no," although it can seem on the surface to be the most logical reason possible. Isn't marriage *supposed* to get rid of loneliness? All of us carry some wounds and holes in our hearts as we move into adulthood. The wounds cry out to be healed, and the holes plead to be filled.

God, in fact, wants these holes to be filled. He is in the *business* of filling them. We all have holes in our hearts, but the truth is that only God can fill the deepest ones. He can use a spouse or friend in great measure to fill some of them, but even then He is still the one working through these people. And although God can use people to fill some of those holes, *we* are not authorized by Him to use people as cures for our emotional sicknesses.

A good marriage is built on wholeness, not desperation. Expectations born of starvation for meaningful relationships will bring only burdens and frustrations to both people. And since we are often drawn to others who have similar emotional pain, *marriage as therapy* becomes *marriage as dysfunction.* And as we said earlier, we have to be especially careful if we are on the rebound.

If you've met your loneliness head-on by developing a satisfactory relationship with God and a comfortable relationship with yourself, you can address the remainder with a rich relationship with another human being. God does put "the lonely [people] in families" (Psalm 68:6 NIV), but no spouse or family can fill a God-sized hole. As it turns out, loneliness—when it is the primary reason for a marriage—is a terrible burden to place on another person.

And one I'm sure you don't want to carry.

Reason #3: You Want Someone to Take Care of You

Skylar was a beautiful, capable, and caring young woman. She had gone through a divorce several years before. She worked hard to raise her only son, at times working two and even three jobs.

I asked her what her vision for her life was. *What is your goal?* "To be taken care of," she said. "I just want someone to take care of me and my son." Although I had heard versions of this answer ("I want to be a 'kept woman,'" "I need a woman who can bring order to my life") many times through the years, I was still stunned.

Some people may seek marriage to avoid taking responsibility. Others may encourage this in order to feel powerful.

If we want to get married to avoid taking responsibility, we're on dangerous ground. Anytime we look to another person—no matter how capable he is—for our protection and security, we are in the wrong place. "Perhaps the most unhealthy myth . . . is: 'My spouse will make me whole' . . . marriage is not a substitute for personal growth."[1]

If we marry a *provider*, our insecurity and fears will still eat at us. They will put unbearable pressure on our spouses. And if that person is a bad choice in any other way, we've made a poor trade for whatever feelings of security the relationship might give us.

One of the most obvious examples of this is where a young person marries a much older spouse. Although the Bible has no guidelines about age differences, this could really be a young person trying to find and marry a father or mother figure. He hopes this older person might take better care of him than his own parent did.

If we are the spouse in the *provider* role, the ground we stand on is no less dangerous. Our need to take care of and oversee the other person's life can lead us to be controlling and bossy. We might even discourage our spouses from growing up and taking personal responsibility because it makes us feel powerful to be so important. Even if our mates cooperate and remain helpless, they will sooner or later—unfairly, we think—resent our control. And we will end up feeling used, as their basic irresponsibility provides fertile soil for new forms of insecurity and fear and even greater demands for our care.

The truth is that God is the ultimate caretaker. He "does not let the righteous go hungry" (Proverbs 10:3; see also Psalm 46:1–2). If we build a relationship of trust with Him, we won't need to look for a fragile human substitute, like the Israelites did when they asked Samuel to give them a king (1 Samuel 12:12–17). And we can add to our own lives by developing skills and abilities through education, intelligent career choices, and right relationships with the many people who surround us. We are told to *add* value, be productive, and keep busy—not to *subtract* value, get by on the work of others, and avoid responsibility.

Dependency is really anti-love. It's like being a parasite or a leech. It's trying to live by draining the life out of someone else. It's acting weak so someone else can feel strong. But excellent relationships are based on power sharing rather than disempowerment, and adding value rather than using it up

In a world that seems so scary, and where it's easy to feel helpless, this desire to be taken care of is understandable. But, physical or financial security might be better sought in a security guard company and a good mutual fund than in a relationship that will make you unhappy and unfulfilled for the rest of your life.

Reason #4: You Want to Escape a Difficult Situation

Alicia had been sexually and emotionally abused by her father. She escaped at first to a boyfriend. They got sexually involved very quickly, in part because she had been trained that way. Then she escaped to college, where she replayed the same kind of relationship with a series of young men. She was frustrated that she kept connecting with men who were angry and unkind.

Inside, Alicia had never really left her abusive home. During her junior year, she married a man who seemed to be the opposite of all the other men in her life, including her father.

Within a year, however, she came to realize that her husband manipulated and used her in the same ways her father had. Her husband, who had looked so fresh-faced and decent, had both lust and anger problems. She thought she had escaped a bad family situation, but this was only an illusion.

Too many people are in terrible living situations. Unfortunately, some of them are in homes that are at least nominally Christian. But marrying to escape these ugly situations is a "cure" that can be worse than the disease.

Why? Because the situation people have grown up in is a model of a home and what they have come to accept as normal. It's easy to repeat the model. And it will be difficult to break the patterns learned in the "empty way of life inherited from the fathers" (1 Peter 1:18) without time for reflection and change and help from a perceptive friend or counselor.

What if we try to choose the *opposite* of what we're living with now? This may lead us to an unsatisfying union—an emotionally flat person in place of the lust, or a spineless person in place of the anger. Even the opposite may really be the same abuse repackaged, with any differences being only superficial. We are too prone to pick out the familiar in others and to live out the same old patterns. Our spouses can end up creating the same havoc in our lives as that caused by the earlier abusers.

We can't escape to a person and hope to be free. The lessons will still need to be learned. Perhaps the most fundamental problem of all is that we have to take ourselves with us wherever we go. If we're just running from a bad situation without learning how it affected us (and, in some cases, how we might have contributed to it), the odds are very high that we'll simply replay it again in our new home. We can become *breakers,* rather than *passers,* of the heritage we've received—but this won't happen without giving deep thought to our behavior (see Proverbs 14:8).

The kind of person who will appeal to you as an escape route will probably look very different from the person who will truly love you after you've spent a few years in deepening and changing your perspective.

By all means, separate yourself from an abusive or degrading situation. Just don't do it by marrying. Don't escape to a person. Instead, escape to a life.

Reason #5: You Want to Solve a Lust Problem

Trent was excited as he pushed three McDonald's french fries into his mouth. "She's *perfect,*" he crowed.

"She's certainly a dynamo," Jared agreed as he picked up his Quarter Pounder.

"I mean, she's intelligent, caring, and going somewhere with her life" Trent said, leaning back against the plastic chair. "I've never met anyone like her."

"You're definitely a lucky guy."

Trent noticed his friend looking away as he sipped his Coke. "What's the matter?"

"Nothing."

"Come on. I've known you too long. Let's hear it."

Jared looked up slowly. "Does she . . . does she know about the . . . pornography . . . ?"

"About the pornography *addiction?*" Trent asked, frowning.

"Well, it's just that we've both wrestled with that stuff for so long, and we've talked about wanting to really win before we get too serious about anyone."

Trent pushed away his tray. "No doubt it's a problem," he admitted. "It's gross, but it's so easy to find and so private. And we've both said it's really a powerful temptation. But," he said, stopping.

"But what?"

"I've been thinking about it, and . . ."

"And . . ."

"I think she's the *cure.*"

"The *cure?*" Jared asked, stunned.

"You bet. It's right there in the Bible. It's 'better to marry than to burn' (1 Corinthians 7:9). Man, I've been burning my whole life. You've dealt with it too. You know what a monster it is to deal with. Now I can finally see the end of that addiction."

Jared leaned back to take in Trent's new insight.

Scary.

Trent's *insight* is one of the most common and stupid ideas floating around the Christian community. The notion is based on a misreading of a verse that's referring to two people who love each other passionately. They long for physical consummation of their unquenchable love. But the verse refers to those who are already feeling a pure and passionate desire toward a *specific* person, not an impure and promiscuous desire toward . . . anyone. If the desire is good and strong, we're told, then don't remain single—this person is *the one.* But if it's strong without being good, we'd better remain single until we can remain pure.

Marriage can *never* solve a lust problem. It's not *able* to do so. Why not? Because only God can solve a lust problem. Only God can control and redirect our desires. And attempting to use marriage as a cure for sin is really an abuse of a relationship.

Burning with lust is different than burning with passion. These are very different *needs* that require very different *solutions.*

Marriage viewed in this incorrect way—as a *silver bullet* against the monster of lust—can actually make a lust problem worse. Why? The person struggling with the problem now has more experience. Lust can still grow, and even be directed at the other person. The lustful person can use outside ideas and fantasies on his spouse. He can also take ideas from the marriage relationship to use in fantasizing about other people.

Jacob was a young man who struggled deeply with sexual issues, including intense homosexual desires at times. He assured his pastor with great confidence that all of his wrong thoughts and desires would come to a dramatic end if he could only find the right woman. His pastor encouraged him not to believe this or put it into practice, but Jacob persisted in his quest.

He got married a year out of high school. The "right" woman finally left him when his wanderings and unloving demands grew too strong for her to bear, and right after Jacob asked her to perform some sexual practice he had learned on the Internet.

It's a bad sign if the other person is pushing for sexual intimacy. And inappropriate premarital intimacy is a problem, not a reason to get married.

Wise people discuss sexuality thoroughly before marriage. This means that we have to be old enough and mature enough to *talk* about it without *doing* it. When talking with engaged couples, I always ask both parties how they know their spouse-to-be has victory with God's help over any lust problems with which he or she has struggled. They are often amazed that the question is asked. In most cases, they haven't given any thought to this crucial issue. The reason I bring it up is not to shock them, but to make sure the couple faces this important matter now—rather than for the rest of their lives in a struggling marriage.

If you ever think about getting married, make *sure* you know the answer to this question.

Reason #6: He or She Is the Fulfillment of Your "Dreams"

Meg thought she had found her dream man. He was active in his youth group, appeared to be a leader, was a serious student, and seemed totally devoted to her. They both threw themselves into the relationship. But after they married and had three children, he began to change. He moved her far away from her family and friends to another state to help start a church.

Soon after their move, he left the church, gave up on God, and divorced her. After three years of wishing and hoping, she finally acknowledged the reality that he wasn't coming back. After two more years she realized he was never who she thought he was in the first place. She realized he had never maintained a long-term relationship with anyone, had never talked about God except at church, and had seemed to harbor an inexplicable rage that came out in traffic and crowds. The seeds were there all along. She just couldn't see them through the "dream."

The likelihood that we can be fooled by our own illusion increases if we've known the other person for a short time. There just hasn't been enough opportunity for us to really see into his or her heart. It's common for the other person to put on a fabulous and convincing front until after the wedding (see Proverbs 26:24–26).

We can be in love with love, not with an actual person, and the other person can play the part of "love." There should be at least a bit of queeziness when we realize that "Satan himself is disguised as an angel of light. . . . his servants also disguise themselves as servants of righteousness" (2 Corinthians 11:14–15). Satan may want to derail your life with a person who is serving him rather than God. Love at first sight can be a delight or a fright. If our way of discovering which one we have is to marry a person and then discover who he is, we've got a good chance of getting the "fright" part.

If this other person is *everything* and becomes the center of our thoughts—even pushing God to the sidelines—then he or she has become an idol who will end up disappointing us. Anyone or anything that consumes us becomes our god. We're headed for disillusionment and unhappiness.

Does this mean we can't be deeply devoted to the other person? Or that we can't carry him in our hearts throughout the day? Or even that we can't dream about him? Of course not. But this is different from letting that person become our god. Our respect and admiration for another person shouldn't move to a level where we see none of his weaknesses or flaws. Or where we exaggerate the potential he has to meet our needs. To have a great marriage, we have to know the difference between devotion and idolatry.

Our first impressions, and even our later perceptions, are not reality. But we have to remember that although dreams are not reality, it can take a long time to wake up. Time is our friend at this point. It allows us to get past the cards and flowers and dream dates and emotional manipulation. It allows us to hear the almost inaudible warnings.

Dreaming about another person? No problem. But to marry the dream? Take a *long* time, and make sure you're awake.

Some dreams can become nightmares.

Reason #7: This Person Is a Real "Find"

Lee was pursued by a continuous stream of young women who encountered him in his college campus ministry. He was intelligent, educated, articulate, and apparently spiritual. He was involved with people, and he was an extremely good listener. He had an ability to make each woman feel that she was the center of his attention.

The problem was that Lee was sexually out of control. For a significant number of women who encountered him, that discovery came too late. Sensitive, caring, emotional times together led to fondling and more. Even then, he seemed so sincere that only one woman blew the whistle on him. Many of the women who had been used by him continued to speak highly of him and recommend him to others.

Lee became a noted psychologist and author, but his sexual problem continued, in spite of his own marriage. Even then, most of the women saw him as a giant who was merely flawed.

The real treasure is usually buried, not *out there* where everyone can see it and admire it. The problem with most of the people on the "most eligible" lists is that they are indeed *eligible.*

The crowd is a judge of popularity, not character. Jesus warns us to "stop judging according to outward appearances; rather judge according to righteous judgment" (John 7:24). Although it's possible that several people might want to marry the same godly person at the same time, the more likely scenario is that the person *seems* attractive because of externals that give no clue to his or her inner character.

Initial attractiveness can hide major flaws. "Imposters," we are told, "will become worse, deceiving and being deceived" (2 Timothy 3:13). If someone seems too good to be true, he just might be.

Once a person's true flaws are known, the number of pursuers will usually decline. If the "flaw" is that the person is willing to be unpopular and stand for truth, some of the shallow followers will be weeded out (see John 6:66). More often than not, though, it's the hidden flaw that proves fatal to a relationship.

The crowd is usually a terrible judge of a person's true character. People tend to value things like "everyone likes him" and "I've never heard anyone say anything negative about her." But in a counter-intuitive moment, the Bible tells us that "*all those* who want to live a godly life in Christ Jesus *will* be persecuted" (2 Timothy 3:12, emphasis added). We should beware of those who have no enemies.

Real love "does not envy" (1 Corinthians 13:4). And the God who is love doesn't design situations that are guaranteed to produce envy. When our eyes are drawn to those who are the most desirable, we've taken our eyes off God. This means we might not see the buried treasure He has so carefully laid up for us.

A lot of people may be pursuing this "perfect person." But remember, if you marry him, you're the only one who will have to live with the flawed person behind the mask.

Reason #8: There May Not Be Another

Jessica was feeling a quiet panic.

She had known Jason for four years, and had been seriously dating him for the last two. They seemed compatible and had fun together. He always treated her courteously. But he seemed directionless. He had been a top student, but this year he had dropped out of all his honors courses. He had gone through half a dozen low-level jobs in a short time. Jessica felt he was really going nowhere, and that a future with him could be a dead end.

But she was a senior. All of her closest friends were seriously committed to a guy. She didn't know anyone else who was unattached and seemed even half as good as Jason. Jessica felt the first wave of panic when she served as maid of honor at the wedding of Heidi, her best friend.

Jessica didn't even *know* any available guys who measured up to Jason. Most of the men at the medical office where she worked were married. Most were also too old, and she had negative feelings about the two single men who were close to her age. She had gone with Heidi to her church's singles group, but the men seemed to be there less for the Bible study than for the chance to pick up women in a better place than a bar.

Jessica felt like her life was slipping away. In the background of a hundred arguments against staying involved with Jason, there was the haunting theme: "There may not be another." So she stuck with him and married him while a junior in college.

Three years later, suffocating from a relationship with a man who only wanted to watch television and go to movies, she met a man at church who stirred all of the feelings she had ever wanted to feel for a man. She did the right thing, and buried those feelings—but she buried them along with her heart.

"Today only" is a very old and effective sales pitch. "This car won't be here tomorrow." "The clothing sale ends tonight." "Do you think another home like this will come along?" People keep using it because it works so often. And it works so often because it appeals to something deep within us that doesn't want to miss a good thing. The sense of lost opportunity can be a powerful force.

But jumping on today's deal is actually the best way to miss the *real* deal when it comes along. The *today only* stuff is a big distraction, structured to stop us at this moment and focus on the bird in the hand. If we buy today, we might not be able to purchase the perfect "product" when it comes along.

We have to remember that "love is patient" (1 Corinthians 13:4). If we really believe God is interested in the details of our lives, that He holds us by the hand and guides us with His counsel, we know that He won't let us miss the deal of a lifetime. If this person is OK—maybe even a decent person, maybe even a great person—but leaves us with too many questions and doubts, it's time to wait. To take no action, except to slow down the train. There are worse things than being married in a life of "quiet desperation"—to quote Henry David Thoreau—but that is small consolation to a heart in a long train ride to emptiness.

Remember that there will always be another if this isn't *the one*.

Reason #9: The Two of You Share "Common Interests"

From the beginning, Maureen and Joel had a sense of destiny about their relationship.

They met when they were picking out the *exact same flavor* of the *exact same low-fat yogurt ice cream*! They both decorated their rooms in the same colors, drove the same type of car, and attended "Shakespeare in the Park" every year. They loved political thrillers and hated soppy romances. Both of them avoided fried foods—except for onion rings at Sonic. They enjoyed tennis and jet skiing but hated spending time at the gym.

So Maureen and Joel got married, and a funny thing happened: their interests changed. Not all of them, and not right away. But over time, the old enthusiasms faded and new ones made their entry. But the old magic was gone. The interests were no longer "common." He liked action movies, and she abhorred the violence. She liked the symphony, and his list of complaints about it was longer than Beethoven's Fifth. He liked to spend evenings alone with her, which she found narrow and stifling. She enjoyed inviting friends over and having a social life, which he found silly and annoying.

Circumstantial evidence can make poor law and poor marriages. Common interests could be a distraction from the deeper and more important business of connecting at the soul. Common interests could be a sign, or they could be a complete distraction.

Part of the problem is that common interests are very fluid and changeable over time. Things that appealed to us ten years ago no longer appeal to us at all, while things we thought we would never be interested in are now an important part of our lives. Many relationships based on those common interests have nowhere to go when those interests change. What will you do if you still like the same things and he doesn't? Or if she still likes the same things and you don't?

But there is an even more serious dimension of this problem. Real life is about *growth*. Successful, satisfying relationships are about enjoying and supporting each others' growth, wherever it leads. The real key is not whether we share common interests, but whether we're capable of loving other persons enough to encourage them and help them in any interests they pursue, whether those things appeal to us or not. In other words, our interest is not in the activity itself, but in the person to whom this activity is important. "Love is not love which alters when it alteration finds," wrote William Shakespeare.

Healthy relationships that are moving toward marriage explore differences. They do not only try to find common ground. Where are we different? What does that mean? How does that make us feel? Does looking at this deepen or distance us? Real life is about unity *and* diversity—a strong soul connection that is expressed in countless and ever-changing ways.

In real life, interests are fluid and changeable. What will you do when they change? Change can lead to either resentment or growth. Will you resist and complain about the "new" person whom he has become? Can you love him even when he is different? *Very* different?

And is there enough about both of you that is the same *at the core*—enough unity around a shared vision and values—to keep that diversity from flying off into chaos?

Reason #10: You Want to Have Children

Tara loved babies.

She had loved babies since she was a little girl. She baby-sat for the neighbors when she was just slightly older than their children. She worked in a day care center during her early high school years and a Montessori preschool for the last year and a half. She wanted—deeply wanted—children of her own. There was an underlying reason. She had some large "holes" in her heart, and she was sure that a house full of children would fill the holes.

But Tara was handicapped by the fact that she had never really liked any guys. She found most of them disgusting. But she determined that she was going to have children the right way, and that her children were going to have a father. Three years after high school, Michael—less loathsome than the other guys—became more the father of her children than the husband of her heart.

The result was one child with crippling spiritual and moral problems, and another one disabled by Tara's dominating and controlling influence. The marriage itself was a piece of cardboard. It lacked any sense of communication, depth, or vitality.

When I hear someone say, "My children are my life" or "I've given up everything for my children," my first thought is *God help those children.* This approach to life is destined to make this parent annoying and destructive to the children.

Baby fever might be a sign of sickness. It may indicate emotional disability. The problem is that wanting children is viewed as a universal good, always worthy of applause. Given the number of children who are abused or dysfunctional, it is amazing that we can keep up such a perspective. Many parents are awful, and an even larger group is unintentionally destructive. Whenever a young woman says, "I want to have a lot of children," experience has taught me to hear *danger, danger.* She may be ordering children as heart salve.

We must evaluate why we want children. If our goal is simply to have some children, we have to ask ourselves *why* we want to have them. If it's just a need to nurture, it can be satisfied in other ways that don't come with the baggage of family life and a spouse who isn't *the one.* We can teach Sunday school, provide day care, become a foster parent, or lead a Scout troop. Even if we're not good parenting material, some of these options will still work. For example, a baby with a mental disability will absorb all of our care and none of our dysfunctions.

Men can get in on this lousy reason as well. Perhaps children, and a pregnant and dependent wife, will make us *feel like a man.* Maybe our lives are out of control, and we need a little army of our own to control (instead of fighting the harder fight of self-control). Some men even use their wives' desire to have children as a way to limit and control their wives, to keep them isolated.

Children are responsibilities, not playthings.

The Bible teaches us that "more are the children of the desolate woman than of her who has a husband" (Isaiah 54:1). This promise can be true for you. Just as God adopts us, so we can *spiritually adopt* children who don't have parents—or at least, parents who love them.

It's amazing how many people feel that having children is also a "calling." It is not. It is a good, even wonderful, part of life for those who approach it as the adventure, the work, and the intimate connection that it can be. If we want to have children to participate in the creation and development of a unique but interdependent human being, we are in the neighborhood of right thinking on this important decision. Having children can be a good part of a richly textured marriage plan.

But marrying just so you can have children? *That* is a very bad plan.

Reason #11: You Feel Pressure to Get Married

Michelle and Adam had been heading toward marriage for almost two years. But for the third time, they were both having doubts.

Michelle's mother went into action again, soothing perceived slights between the two, telling Michelle what a wonderful person Adam was, telling Adam that his doubts were nothing more than those that every man has before such a big decision.

As it turned out, this mother was driven by several forces that were not working in the best interest of Michelle and Adam. She was concerned about the quality of the men Michelle had spent time with before Adam. She saw this as an opportunity to get her daughter settled with a good person. Even worse, she was vicariously "marrying" Adam through her daughter, largely because of her own disappointing marriage. She wanted this young man in her family.

Years later, Adam and Michelle's marriage was still wrestling with fundamental questions that should have been resolved before the marriage occurred—if, in fact, it was ever a good idea for the two people to get married to each other.

Pressure can be open or subtle, heavy-handed or gentle, self-centered or full of good intentions. It can be external or internal. It can come from parents, brothers, sisters, friends, coworkers, or people at school or church. It can also come from an indistinct feeling that all of our friends are getting married, and that we are the only ones not sharing in this "bliss." The feeling that we are falling behind is normal, but acting on that feeling can produce problems. This can build as we get older, and all of the good, marriageable people seem to be taken. No one wants to be left behind.

The pressure can even come from the other person, our possible spouse-to-be. It can be as crude as the pressure for intimate

relations ("if you really loved me . . ."), but is at its most dangerous when it is cast in poetic terms ("you know we were made for
each other," "you've seen all the signs that God is the one who put
us together," "think of all we can do for God and others when
we've got our own home"). The *I-swear-I-love-you* approach con-
tradicts the biblical command not to use verbal manipulation.[3] If
we're wise, pressure from the other will stir the *opposite* reaction. It
will alarm us. Why is he doing this? What's behind this push? Why
can't she wait?

Christians and churches can add to this problem by becoming
blessing machines and pushing marriage as some sort of universal
"good." Based on a reading of Ephesians 5, many people talk about
marriage as a picture of the relationship between Christ and the
church. At its best, marriage is certainly this. But it doesn't happen
automatically. Good marriages are grown and developed into this
kind of relationship.

Parents can get in on the pressure act in two different ways.
They can pressure us not to marry the person who really is *the
one.* But they can also pressure us to marry a person who isn't *the
one,* for a variety of unhealthy reasons. Maybe they think marriage will settle us down. Maybe they think we ought to get married to a certain person because he or she is the best of the lot
they've seen us with. Maybe they just want us out of the house.
We have no guarantee that our parents have any special insight
here. We should listen to what they say and then check it out. We
should trust but verify.

If all of our friends are getting married, we would spend our
time praying for them rather than seeking a marriage of our own.
Love truly doesn't envy (see 1 Corinthians 13:4). Our friends will
need every one of those prayers. One young woman who had been
pressured into a bad marriage told her best friend, "You were the
one who was really smart. You waited until the right time and the
right person, rather than just jumping in like I did because it
seemed the thing to do."

Marriage is such an important decision that we shouldn't do it because of pressure of any kind. Take your time and think hard. When there's no pressure and you're still sure, you're probably on the right path. At least you're a lot safer.

Reason #12: He or She Acts Like You Are the Center of the Universe

Angie had never felt so cared for.

Derek overwhelmed her with his attention and care. He remembered all of the special occasions and celebrated them with creativity and thoughtfulness. On her birthday, he took the afternoon off to spend with her. They shared lunch at an outdoor Polynesian restaurant and dinner at a little café in the renovated center of downtown. They talked, laughed, and enjoyed the smallest of details. He finished the day by giving Angie a beautiful bracelet.

He did more. He created their own "holidays"—the anniversary of the day when they met, the day when they first decided to "go together," and the time when they first discussed the possibility of marriage. He called her every day, sent cards, and made a point of praising her in front of everyone. Derek treated her like a movie princess.

There was only one problem. Angie didn't love Derek. She loved his care and attention but felt nothing for Derek himself. And there were things that concerned her—how he emphasized the importance of the relationship to his own well-being, the way he avoided talking about problems, his disinterest in socializing with anyone else. But where would she ever find another man who loved her this much?

No one has ever been loved too much. Because of this, all of us are prone to yield to an onslaught of care and good will. When another person acts like we're "it," the very center of his universe, it can feel so delightful that we never want it to stop. We can blind ourselves to the realities of our own feelings and to the potential of the relationship itself.

We might be another person's center, but we have to remember that one type of center is a bull's-eye. He might end up putting an arrow through our heart. When he stops all that attention and walks away, the depression will seem deeper because the mountain had been so high.

Another type of center is chewy—and she could be softening us up to munch on our souls. Her devotion to us might really be devotion to herself. She may be telling us what *we* want to hear so she can get what *she* wants. If she seems overly concerned about her need for our commitment, she may be missing the truth that love "is not selfish" (1 Corinthians 13:5).

Avoiding serious discussions by flooding us with attention and activity could be an introduction to empty evenings for many decades to come. And we should be leery of those who don't want to socialize or have other friends because no genuine relationship has ever existed in a vacuum. What's up? Does she want to control us? Does he want to keep us from seeing his social flaws?

The worst of it all if you marry this type of person is that the attention will likely evaporate when the prize—you—is won. If it is a quest, the drive is to do whatever it takes to achieve the goal, but not to do it any longer. Why work so hard when you've achieved your goal? You could find that you've sold your life for a self-esteem "high."

And you are worth a lot more than that.

Conclusion

Are there good reasons to get married? Certainly! Are there lousy reasons to get married? Absolutely! The key is to marry for all of the right reasons and none of the wrong ones.

With God's help and some clear thinking, you can find the key.

Discussion Questions

On Your Own

- *Ask Yourself:* Have I ever heard people using the reasons in this chapter as the basis for their marriages?
- *Ask Your Parents:* Could you give me an example to illustrate each of the reasons given in this chapter? What other lousy reason for getting married have you heard people use?
- *Ask Your Youth Pastor or Pastor:* Would you look through the list in this chapter and probe deeply to see if any of these things might be driving my current relationship with another person? Would you give me examples from your experience of people who married for any of these reasons? Will you give me as much detail as you can so I can see whether I'm being driven by any of these reasons?

Together

- *Ask Yourselves:* How would I rate myself and this relationship on each of these reasons on a one-to-ten scale, with one meaning "no possibility that this reason is a motivating factor" and ten meaning "this reason is driving me toward marriage"?
- *Ask Each Other:* (Share your ratings with each other and seriously discuss anything you rated higher than one). Would you please tell me about the other important relationships in your life, especially those with your parents, siblings, and close friends? Would you tell me how you feel those relationships have hurt you, and how those hurts feel today? Would you please tell me about your struggles with lust? Would you tell me how the Enemy attacks you in your thought life, and how this has affected your past relationships with other people? Would you share with me what level of victory you've achieved in this area, and how you achieved it?

A man may be a fool and not know it,
but not if he is married.
H. L. Mencken

twelve problem people to avoid

chapter 7

"Are you happy or married?"

This question, posed by Moe of the Three Stooges while acting as a door-to-door census taker, is funny because there is so much truth behind it.

A lot of things in life can make us miserable. But for many people, it takes marriage to really create a little hell on earth. A lot of people who are relatively happy as single people end up unhappy after marriage.

There are many reasons for this, but one of the biggest is that you marry the wrong person—not just someone who is less than your ideal, but someone who is really *wrong*.

We're all sinners, but if you get involved with someone who has really caved in to one of the problems we're going to lay out for you in this chapter, you are in a world of hurt.

The line separating good and evil passes not through states, nor between political parties either—but right through every human heart.
Aleksandr Solzhenitsyn
in *The Gulag Archipelago*

The "Fix-It" Illusion

If you're attracted to another person, it will be very hard to see these problems for what they are. You might even get past the romance and charm and attractiveness and see that they have a problem. That's good.

But it's not enough. Not even close.

If you want to avoid getting slaughtered by this problem, you've got to see it for what it is, in all of its full-blown ugliness. You can't afford to play games on this. If it's really bad, it's likely to get a whole lot worse.[1] These problems won't just go away. Even if the person whom you marry is a Christian, it will take a focused resolve to access God's grace so you can get this thing down to manageable size.

But if you see this problem and realize how bad it is, this is still not enough. If you force yourself to think about this, you're letting your head keep up with your heart. That's very good. Just seeing problems clearly and thinking about them in a realistic way is hard to do—but you can do it with God's help. He is stronger than your hormones, stronger than attraction, and stronger than romance. He doesn't want you to fall head over heels for a bad spouse. He'll help you make the hard decision.

What is the hard decision?

The hard decision is not trying to fix the person. It's not trying to fix his problem. One reason is that you can't do it. You don't have the power. Even *God* won't make a person change. This person could change if he wanted to. A lot of people never want to.

Another reason is that you are the wrong person to make the attempt. "But I love him," you might say. "I'm the perfect person to change him. My *love* for him will change him." These are wonderful sentiments. They show a good heart. But there's only one problem: You are too wrapped up to tell it like it is, to hurt him as badly as he needs to be "hurt," to be willing to risk the loss of the relationship if you expose the evil or weakness. You can't be as objective as you need to be, because your love is a very subjective force.

A third reason is that the person may not want to change. She might *like* the way she is. She may say, "I hate that I get so angry so easily, and I'm going to change," but that could simply be nice words to camouflage an evil heart. *Of course* she will say that. *Of course* she won't say, "I know I'm rotten, but take it or leave it. I like being nasty, and I have no intention of changing." She is smart enough to know that almost anyone would make a run for it if he heard the truth.

Of course this person needs someone to help her with her problem. But if you are romantically involved with her, or even leaning in that direction, *you are not that someone.*

The hard decision is to walk away from the problem person.

Or run.

Who Are Problem People?

Let's start by being honest: *Everyone has problems.* If we wait for perfect people to have as friends or to marry, humanity will come to an end.

As you read through the rest of this chapter, you might find yourself thinking that you are struggling with one or more of these problems. God will honor your humility. Ask for help in these areas. The last thing you want is for one of these issues to grow up in your own life and turn *you* into one of the twelve problem people.

And that's what sin does. It grows up. We're told that "temptation comes from the lure of our own evil desires. These evil desires lead to evil actions, and evil actions lead to death" (James 1:14–15 NLT). Everyone is tempted. Our own sinful nature, even when we are Christians, can draw us away and entice us. If we give in, the evil desire gives birth to sin. When that puppy is fully grown, it's a hound of hell. It's major-league death.

Now there's something we know about death from the Bible. The Israelites were told, "Whoever touches the dead body of anyone will be unclean for seven days" (Numbers 19:11; see also Numbers 5:2; 6:6; 9:6–7, 10; 19:13 NIV). Of course this had a

111

practical application—to keep people from spreading disease. But isn't there a spiritual application as well? Doesn't this tell us that death is contagious? That getting too close to death will defile us? That *if we hang out with dead people, we'll end up dead?*

At the end of a verse that tells us to be merciful and to try to help others, Jude includes a warning that mercy should be mixed with fear, "hating even the garment defiled by the flesh" (Jude 23). Don't get too close to corruption, he says, even if you're trying to do a good deed.

There are problems that go beyond the usual imperfections all of us have. These problems can indicate a spirit that is not right with God and a soul that is severely damaged. The serious problems that people bring from their past can be difficult to resolve and can affect their future relationships in both obvious and subtle ways.

These problems don't disqualify people from marriage—unfortunately. They should. No person who is a slave to any of these problems is ready for a good relationship with anyone else. They are guaranteed to bring you great harm.

These problems have to be discussed, honestly faced, and corrected in the hands of God and caring Christians before a person is ready to enter into a decent, sound relationship.

The alternative, dating and marriage as therapy ("my love will turn her around"), is an illusion. Marriage as a cure for these severe problems in others can fail on many grounds.

First, only God can fix these problems, with a willing and repentant person. This may happen in your lifetime, and it may never happen.

Second, we can actually end up adding to the problem, as we get between the problem person and God and perhaps prevent him from having to own up to his problem. He won't get better if he delegates the problem to you, and you end up making excuses for it.

Third, her problems and frustrations can build as she realizes that the marriage isn't fixing things. You told her you would love her *no matter what*. Well, this is no-matter-what time. She will wonder if your love is defective, since it didn't make her better.

Fourth, we can end up being victimized by his unresolved problem as we try to keep up with—or to break free from—the dance of death. Why are we pulling away? Why don't we love him just as he is? What's wrong with our love? We can end up feeling guilty, even though he is the one with the problem.

Finally, she may have a strong wall of resistance to change. She has been ignoring God. Why shouldn't she ignore you?

What if the other person claims to be a Christian and says that he loves you? Won't that be enough? No. Because he says he is a Christian but there is no fruit, it is probably a sham (see Matthew 7:16–20). And even if he is a Christian, he may not really love you. It may instead be a desperate need or desire that he is calling "love."

And even if she is a Christian and loves you, that may not be enough, by itself, to give you a decent long-term relationship. These problems are difficult to resolve. Marriage is hard enough for two growing Christians.

It's the valley of the shadow of death when you're married to one of these people.

The Twelve Problem People to Avoid

There are probably dozens of people in your church who wish they had been exposed to this section of the book before they got married. Ignorance isn't bliss, and they've paid for not knowing this. But you will know it. And I hope you won't forget it.

There are twelve really ugly expressions of sin. These problems, based on the Sermon on the Mount (see Matthew 5–7), are as follows.

1. Anger (See Matthew 5:21–26)

Allison told two of her friends that she was already dreaming about being married to Nick. But Allison was secretly worried about Nick's temper. He blew up in traffic and pounded on the steering wheel while calling other drivers names—sometimes foul ones. He would even trade comments with them. If she was a few minutes late, he would fume and make cutting remarks. Sometimes he would stay mad the entire evening. He verbally assaulted his little brother whenever he came into the room. Kristi, her best friend, had asked Allison about his anger, but Allison had denied it was that bad. Nick was too good a catch to lose over a little temper tantrum or two. She was sure he would calm down as he got a little older.

Allison is in a dream world. It's not that we shouldn't marry someone who gets angry, because any of us can do that. But we are commanded not to associate with a person who is easily angered (see Proverbs 22:24). This means a person who explodes easily, nurtures anger, and is full of contempt and degrading comments about other people. Allison isn't letting herself see that the way Nick treats family, friends, and strangers is the way he will ultimately treat her. Do you want to raise your children with people like Nick?

2. Addiction (See Matthew 5:27–30)

Rachel lived for her music and favorite television programs. She insisted on putting her albums into Austin's CD player in his car, and she basically zoned out while the music was playing. She would never miss her TV programs even for special events, even though Austin offered to program her VCR. It seemed to Austin that she lived on sweets for days at a time, especially when school was maxing her out. *This will all pass,* Adam thought. *She'll grow out of this.*

But Rachel might never grow out of these addictions. They might get worse, or she might trade them in for some other escape. Addictions are designed by the Enemy to relieve pressure and fill our emptiness. They include lust (the wandering eye), gluttony (food as a filler of soul-holes), drunkenness (alcohol, drugs), and other things that can turn into chains if we overuse them (like sleep, television, music, sports, shopping, spending). They can be pointed directly at the other person in an addiction to sexual activity (based on sexual brokenness and confusing sex with intimacy) or an addiction to the person (by focusing on the relationship as the escape).

Another little twist: People who can't control themselves still feel the need to be in control. So guess what? They may try to satisfy that need by controlling *you*. In fact, they can try to use their addiction as a way of controlling you—by making you care for them 24/7 or by blaming you for their problems.

3. A Littered Trail (See Matthew 5:31–32)

The last three months had been the best of Tim's life. Ashley had not only started paying attention to him; she was going out with him only. She was the most beautiful girl in the class, and every guy he knew was calling him "lucky." He had awakened in the middle of the night several times dreaming that she had dumped him. Occasionally he had the thought that she had already had four different serious boyfriends in the last year and a half. This made him feel partly like he'd been picked out of the crowd and partly very insecure. He hadn't seen her at school for two days, and she hadn't called him back last night, but . . .

Tim is probably in serious trouble. Ashley's problem could be fear of closeness, or it could be more sinister—enjoying using guys and tossing them aside. If the other person has a string of broken relationships in the past, we need to dig to see if there is a pattern. Did they cause the problems? Did she learn anything from them? Has she succumbed to "victimitis"? Does she refuse to accept responsibility? Has scapegoating become a habit? When her problem is always somebody else's fault, that is the problem. It might be that she was always dumped by the other person—but why? Maybe there's a good reason. She can learn the right lessons from her past wounds and failures—or she can learn the wrong ones, and apply them to you.

4. Verbal Cunning (See Matthew 5:33–37)

"I'd never ask you to do this if I wasn't totally committed to you forever," Patrick whispered, just inches from Cassidy's ear. "I've never even thought about that with any other girl."

Cassidy looked out the window of the car into the soft spring night. "I don't know . . ." she said, wavering.

"We've been going out for two years," he said, "and you've never even seen me look at another girl, have you?"

Slowly, Cassidy looked into his tender blue eyes.

"Just close," he suggested, his tone sensitive and genuine. "Not all the way."

Cassidy closed her eyes. She knew she was at a turning point in her life.

Beware the person who uses verbal manipulation ("I *swear* I love you"; "if you loved me you would do that"), verbal control ("you're not really serious about that"; "you know you shouldn't do that"), or verbal coercion ("if you had a servant's heart you'd do that for me"; "if you don't agree, I'm leaving"). If he doesn't respect you enough to let you make your own decisions, he doesn't really love you; he just loves what you can do for him. You should also steer clear of those with hidden agendas (they don't say what they mean or mean what they say), and those you catch in lies (see John 8:44). This isn't limited to either guys or girls; anyone can use his or her tongue to trap other people. And especially watch out for the person who beats you or other people to death with the Bible. The Bible is a sword (see Ephesians 6:17), not a club.

5. Scorekeeping (See Matthew 5:38–42)

"You see what I mean, don't you Jeff?" Megan persisted.

"I don't know, Meg," he answered. "It seems like you're being a little hard on her."

Megan was furious. "That's the third time in this conversation that you've taken *her* side," she fumed. "Don't you understand? She didn't invite me to her party. I thought we were friends. I'll never invite her to anything else again."

"Meg, you . . ." he started, but her look wilted him. *That's four*, he could almost hear her saying.

Scorekeepers are a tough lot. They are always keeping track of what they think you owe them, and they can be quite unhappy when you don't deliver. This problem can take several forms: the *lex talionis*—eye for an eye—form (they give back what they get), the best-defense form (they think it's a good offense, so they attack before someone else attacks them), the win/lose form (they fight to win every discussion or argument), or the revenge form (they look for chances to even the score). Scorekeepers can also be bankers (they only give you something if they can get it back), evaluators (they measure others by their usefulness), and sentinels (they work hard not to be "cheated"). Often, they are also really cheap, and watch every penny to make sure others are paying at least their share (or more).[2] It is very difficult for a relationship to survive scorekeeping, and you can rest assured that such a mate will do it with you.

6. Warring (See Matthew 5:43–48)

"Let's face it, he's just a jerk," Will almost spit the words. "I felt like going up to the front of the room and throwing him out the window."

"Will," Lindsey pleaded softly, "I don't think he was trying to embarrass you. He just asked why you hadn't read the chapters."

Will looked at her like she was a toddler. "Of course he was trying to embarrass me," he insisted, shaking his head. "He's been after me since the start of the semester. I hate that jerk. I think I'm going to see if I can get a couple of the guys to write complaint letters to the office about him. Maybe we can get him in trouble, or even fired. I think Tony will do it."

Lindsey tried to take his hand. "Tony told me he's really trying to get a good grade in that class," she said, "so I'm not sure he'll want to get involved."

Will pushed her hand away. "He'll do it," he said, looking up, "or I'll show him."

Some people approach life with a confrontational attitude. You should notice how they define an enemy. Is it anyone who disagrees with them? Do they appreciate constructive criticism, or do they attack the person who tried to help? Do they return evil for good (like running down someone who told them an uncomfortable truth)? Do supposed enemies (like a tough teacher) dominate their conversation? Are they always at odds with their parents ("my Dad is just trying to control me")? Do they care about non-family members? The Bible says you are better off living in the corner of a roof than to live in a house with a quarrelsome person.[3] If this person likes to fight and you get entangled with him or her, we know what you'll be doing on several thousand nights of a very . . . marriage.

7. Pride (See Matthew 6:1–18)[4]

At first, Lauren had thought Paul was the coolest Christian she'd ever known. It seemed like every week he would tell the group about his experiences witnessing about his faith to everyone he met. He also shared with them about his volunteer activities, how he'd helped the men's group on a Thanksgiving mission to the inner city, and how he had given some of his own money to one of the families. He prayed at length with the group and had done it so often that the youth pastor was now asking him to lead prayer regularly. Just last night, Paul had told them about his intention to do a two-day fast to pray about the Middle East.

It all seemed so good. He was so enthusiastic and out in front of everyone. Lauren was spending more and more time with him. And yet . . . *And yet what?* she asked herself. Why was she uncomfortable? Was it because Paul was always the center of his stories, the hero? Or was it that it was so important to him to give the group all the details? She didn't know. But she was definitely uncomfortable.

Nothing can be more appealing to us than someone who talks about faith and spiritual things, who seems to be doing something, who seems bold and sure. It can be a sign of depth. But it can also be a sign of cancerous pride. We need to beware of people who are the stars of their own show, who care more about their public image than the actual work. These people brag about their generosity and talk a lot about their exploits for God ("I led four people to the Lord"). Even their prayers are intended to impress others. Some masquerade as martyrs, making much of their "sacrifices." Pride is very hard to bear over the long term (like a marriage). We're told that "The Lord tears down the proud man's house" (Proverbs 15:25 NIV)—and you'll be in it if you marry him. There's a difference between boldness and pride. Lauren can feel the difference. So can you.

8. Greed (See Matthew 6:19–24)

Kevin was still enjoying his times out with Brianna. Mostly. She was really pretty and energetic, and seemed to like him a lot. He did get a little tired of her preferred activity out, which was shopping. At first, he was happy to pay for her food and drinks, but it bothered him that she never had any money with her and never offered to pay. And he knew that both of them were getting about the same amount of money every week from part-time jobs and parents. She would look at something in a store until he asked her if she wanted it. Her answer was something like, "Yes, but I don't have enough money with me." He was spending zero on himself and thinking about working a few more hours on the weekend.

The kicker was last night, when they went out for his birthday. He ended up paying for the dinner, and Brianna had only given him a card and some brownies she had made. He felt guilty and selfish that he'd wanted more, but . . .

Kevin is in for a long, hard, frustrating time if he continues with Brianna. He is destined to feel used, which is certain to lead to resentment and anger. You should watch out for people who don't have the wisdom to say "enough" (see Colossians 3:5). They might be selfish (want to spend it on themselves) or stingy (don't want to spend it on others, probably including you). One clue is if they're always talking about *stuff*. And do they speak up when they are *under*charged? Or do they brag about getting away with paying less? Another giveaway is when giving money or things to others seems to hurt them. They can also be greedy about our time and attention. You will never be able to earn enough or give enough to satisfy a greedy person. Hide your wallet or purse, and find a friend who understands generosity.

9. Fretting (See Matthew 6:25–34)

"It'll be OK," John tried to comfort Mallory. "You'll do fine. You always do fine on tests."

She looked at him with frustration, like he was a little child. "You just don't understand," she said. "I missed two days last week. I got the notes, but I feel out of it. I know I'm going to mess up, and there goes my *A*."

John started to say something else but stopped. Mallory was always worried about something—what people thought of her, whether she was too fat, her health, getting killed in an accident, grades, whatever. And whenever he tried to calm her down, she got frustrated and angry with him. It was like she *enjoyed* worrying about things. But that was too weird. *Surely she doesn't want to worry about everything.*

But John might be wrong. Mallory might want to worry, and she might even *enjoy* worrying. You should know that there are people who worry about sickness and death, about losing what they have, about being abandoned or betrayed, about whether God will take care of them, about the future—and about you and your trustworthiness. They will always be worried about you not liking them or leaving them or betraying them. They will have to put God's kingdom second because their real energy is spent on this life. So here's the question: If a person isn't happy or secure, will close friendship or marriage make her so? Will *you?* Not likely.

10. Judging (See Matthew 7:1–5)

"I can't believe they went to that movie," Braydon said to Tessa, shaking his head, "I mean, they've got people living together in that movie like it's normal or something. I don't think we should go out with them anymore."

Tessa was alarmed. "Emily is my best friend," she argued.

"Emily is a *sicko* if she goes to movies like that," he said with absolute certainty. Braydon enjoyed commenting on other people's choices and mistakes. But Tessa noticed that he didn't take criticism well at all. Mostly, he tore up her friends.

Nobody's ever good enough for him, Tessa thought.

Some people are judging machines. These people have plenty of condemnation to go around, while they dispense mercy with an eyedropper. They have all the answers, and they spend their time "fixing" others and criticizing them for problems (that they themselves usually have in abundance). They are often meddlers, intruding into other people's business. They'll often do it in the name of God (which is definitely taking His name in vain). And they almost always have a thin skin—criticize them at your peril.[5] By the way, Tessa is right. No one is good enough for Braydon. Including her. Time to find a friend who celebrates life and people.

11. Being Undiscerning (See Matthew 7:6)

"Why did you tell her that?" Sean asked, choking.

"I don't know . . . she's my friend, I guess," Whitney offered. "I don't think she'll spread it around."

Sean looked at her in disbelief. "Are you kidding? She's got the biggest mouth in the group. You know she's going to tell everyone. So much for confidentiality. I thought I could trust you."

Whitney was in tears. "You can trust me," she said. "You know I'm on your side."

But the problem is that Sean can't trust Whitney. Why not? Because she isn't trustworthy. She doesn't know who she shouldn't trust or when to keep things to herself. Undiscerning people talk to anyone who will listen (your marriage will have no privacy), trust everyone including swindlers (you'll go broke), don't know when to walk away (you'll be up to your neck in problems you can do nothing about), and keep going back for more abuse (they've been trained to like it, but you'll hate it). There is a fundamental weight of irresponsibility that both of you will be crushed under. By trusting everyone with everything, people like this ironically end up unable to be trusted with anything.

12. Hypocrisy (See Matthew 7:15–23)

Tray was the best guy Brigette had ever known. He was a leader in every group he belonged to. She had helped him plan the last fund-raiser for the youth group and had worked long hours for him, organizing their recent camping trip for sixty kids. But she hadn't been able to get something from that week at camp out of her mind. She was coming back from a walk with Teresa when she heard some guys laughing behind one of the buildings. As they got closer, she could hear them talking about the girls in the group—how hot some were, how ugly others were. She and Teresa stopped, transfixed, and listened. But when Teresa's name came up as one of the "uglies," Brigette grabbed her arm and walked away quickly. She felt so bad for Teresa. But something was even worse. *Tray was the one who had insulted her friend!*

Brigette has discovered that there are two kinds of leaders—real leaders who practice what they preach and hypocrites who want *others* to practice what they preach. These people love themselves instead of others. They demand what they won't give. They suffer from the tailgate syndrome ("back off if you're behind me or get out of the way if you're in front"). They are a one-way street.

They expect you to listen to them, but they'll interrupt you all the time. You have to make sure you are looking at their actions and not just listening to their words. Sheep words can mask wolf actions.

But if you watch these people long enough, their actions will give them away. Not all of their actions—they'll do some good deeds to make themselves believable. But only some. If you watch closely, they'll do something that reveals who they are. Too many Little Red Ridinghoods see the teeth and still marry the wolf instead of running for dear life. Brigette should realize that, sooner or later, she's going to be Tray's target.

There you have it. Twelve problems that we should be aware of in a human being. Keep your eyes open. Trust your instincts. Use your common sense. And listen hard to the Holy Spirit.

The Bible has a strong warning and some strong advice for us when it comes to these kinds of people: "I wrote to you in a letter *not to associate* with sexually immoral people—by no means referring to this world's immoral people, or to the greedy and swindlers, or to idolaters; otherwise you would have to leave the world. But now I am writing you *not to associate* with anyone who bears the *name* of brother who is sexually immoral or greedy, an idolater or a reviler, a drunkard or a swindler. *Do not even eat* with such a person" (1 Corinthians 5:9–11, emphasis added).

If we're not supposed to associate with people like this, or even to eat with them, my guess is that we're probably not supposed to *marry* them.

God doesn't want you to be trapped by any of these people. The Bible is full of warnings about them. Jesus spent a long sermon talking about these problems. Why? So we can avoid these problems in our own lives and avoid getting close to people who have made these problems their way of life.

Don't get close to people with these problems. The price is too high.

Hard Facts

The prophet Haggai asked some very interesting (and sort of weird) questions of the Israelites. Take a minute to look them up, in Haggai 2:11–14. What do you think? Does this talk about carrying meat in your clothes and people who have touched defiling meat make any sense? Does it have any meaning for us today?

Could it be that Haggai is telling us that the holy things don't rub off on the unholy? That the clean doesn't purify the defiled? That, instead, it's the other way around? That the unholy and defiled rubs off on the holy, and causes it to be defiled, too?

There are some people who refuse to be fixed, no matter how much we love them and care about them and do things for them. We don't want to write people off, but just because they need help doesn't mean that you're the one to give it in a *marriage*. Trying to help a dysfunctional person when your heart is wrapped up with him or her is mission impossible.

So if you want to be successful in relationships and in your life, you have to face a few hard facts:

- There are rotten people in the world.
- Some of them are your age.
- Some of them you probably already know.
- Some of them are from the opposite sex.
- At least one of them will probably be attractive to you in some way.
- The Enemy may have sent this person to you to mess up your life.
- You can't "fix" these people.
- If you ignore the teaching and warnings, they *will* mess up your life.

I wish these things weren't true. But they are. The good news is, you don't have to be ignorant. You don't have to be a dummy.

You can avoid these people and have the time of your life.

And if you see one of these problems in yourself, you can weed it out of your life before you ever get into a serious relationship. Remember, another person can't change you. But *you* can.

Discussion Questions

On Your Own

- *Ask Yourself:* Do I understand the kinds of people I should avoid? Do I know how to recognize them? Do I see any of these problems in my friends? What am I doing to make sure I don't get trapped by any of these people, in friendship or in marriage? What is inwardly pushing me to want to date this person?

- *Ask Your Parents:* Would you go through each of the twelve problem people in this chapter and give me any extra advice you have on them? Can you give me examples from your own life on any of these? Do you think any of my friends fit any of these categories?

- *Ask Your Youth Pastor or Pastor:* Would you teach me and the rest of our group about these kinds of people and how to recognize them? Will you warn me if you see me getting involved with any of them? Why do you think these people haven't changed?

Together

- *Ask Each Other:* Have I been like any of the people listed in this chapter? Have you been like any of them? Has this always been a problem? What have you done to change? Do either of our parents struggle with any of these problems? (Remember, these things often get passed down.)

Recognizing
a Good Match
for a Great Marriage
Part 3

If you are afraid of loneliness, don't marry.
Anton Chekhov

the best reasons for getting married
chapter 8

Here is an interesting verse from the Bible that I thought you would enjoy: "If anyone thinks he is acting improperly toward the virgin he is engaged to, and if she is getting along in years and he feels he ought to marry, he should do as he wants. He is not sinning. They should get married" (1 Corinthians 7:36).

Now, what this verse is saying is good for many married people to know.

Maybe they sort of wandered into a marriage. "Acting improperly" could mean they are pushing the intimacy boundaries, or it could mean that if he doesn't marry her he's just stringing her along. Maybe "getting along in years" is saying that she's now old enough to get married, or maybe it's also implying that she thinks it's time to tie the knot. If this relationship just has some sort of momentum, it's OK for them to get married.

Love is merely a madness; and, I tell you, deserves a dark house and a whip as madmen do: and the reason why they are not so punished and cured is that the lunacy is so ordinary that the whippers are in love too.
William Shakespeare

If they get married for any or all of these reasons, it's not a sin. Now that's good news. Even if you don't have great reasons to get married, you can still get married and not have it be a sin. You don't have to ask anyone to forgive you. You don't have to apologize.

But you still might have to cry.

The Bible is a very practical, real-world book. God understands that most people are not going to marry for the best reasons. But as long as they're not doing it for the *wrong* reasons, they can marry and it won't be considered a sin.

Saying, "Well, we didn't get married for the best of reasons, but we've tried to be good for each other" is a little like running a business with this slogan: *We're No Worse Than Anyone Else.*

Sort of makes you want to shop there, doesn't it?

I don't want you to avoid only terrible marriages or miserable marriages or poor marriages. I want you to avoid mediocre marriages and average marriages and *pretty good* marriages as well. That's the whole point of this book, and a specific focus of this chapter and chapters 9 and 10.

This chapter is specifically for those who are seriously considering something more than friendship. But it's OK to read it even if you're far away from that point, even if you're fourteen or sixteen or eighteen. Why? Because having the right reasons to get married clearly in your head will leave less room for the stupid reasons.

And you want to be brilliant. You want to have the best marriage of the twenty-first century. Why not? Someone has to have it. Why not you?

The Best Reasons to Get Married

Let's explore together the best reasons to yield our singleness.

- You have found a soul match.
- Your soul match can become a life partner.
- The life partner will enhance your spiritual life.
- You will enhance his or her spiritual life.

- You have interdependence.
- Love can be heard and absorbed both ways.
- Your differences are complementary rather than destructive.
- This person really is *the one*.

Let's look at each of these in a little more detail.

You have found a soul match

A soul match starts with the principles and clues we discussed in chapter 3, "Recognizing a Person Worth Knowing and Marrying." If that chapter isn't fresh in your mind, go over it again.

But a soul match is even more than this. A soul match is a person who knows you in a way that even close friends don't.

An outstanding example of this in the Bible is the deep relationship between David and Jonathan. In a stunning statement, far beyond what most men even get close to, they make a covenant of friendship. It says that "Jonathan had David reaffirm his oath out of love for him, because he loved him as he loved himself."[1] These two guys developed a one-in-a-thousand friendship. A covenant friendship. A soul match that honored God and made them more spiritual men.

Now here's the deal: It's just as likely that a soul match could be a friend of the same sex rather than a potential marriage partner of the opposite sex. Maybe even *more* likely, *depending on how you define it*. Why? My daughter Laura, a multitalented and degreed person who teaches high school as this is being written, says it this way:

> If by "soul mate," you mean someone who shares your values, principles, vision, and passion for God, then it may be hoped that *all* your closest relationships will fit the description . . . but if you mean someone who shares your temperament, your interests, your social style, your exact goals and ministries, your career, or an

ability to read your mind and do for you exactly
what you secretly wish to have done for you at
any given moment, you are looking for someone
who does not exist. It is possible that you may
find someone who shares your exact interests
and can read your mind to some extent, but he
or she will probably be a person of your own
gender. If you're looking for camaraderie when
you use the term *soul mate,* get yourself a friend,
not a spouse.

So let's agree. When we use the term *soul match,* we're talking
about someone who is very different from you in many ways, but
somehow has an astonishing appreciation for, and identification
with, your soul—your values, principles, vision, and passion for
God, as well as your joys, feelings, emotions, and struggles.

A person who is a soul match deeply understands your interests and talents and strengths in a way that no one else does—
perhaps not even you. And this person deeply understands your
weaknesses and doubts and fears, because these things are somehow lodged in his or her own soul as well.

Christie is very fortunate. She has worked hard at relationships
and at caring about people, and she believes she has three soul
matches—Abby, Jared, and Ben. All of them are seniors, and all of
them know one another.

Your soul match can become a marriage partner

So where does Christie stand on the possibility of partnership?

Abby has been Christie's best friend since they were in second
grade. There is no question that they are a soul match. Unlike
most friendships of youth, this one has an honest-to-goodness
shot at lasting through college and beyond—maybe for the rest of
their lives. But Abby and Christie are both girls, so obviously they
can't get married.[2] They realize that a soul match is a great gift

from God, and they can enjoy their friendship for the next hundred years.

Christie has never known a guy quite like Jared. He is sensitive, thoughtful, and caring. In some ways he is a male version of Abby, although he is also very masculine and even more energetic. She dated him seriously for over a year, until they had a fight that they were never quite able to get past. They hang out together, but more as best friends than as any kind of romantic partner. They love talking about God and the Bible and life. They are so close that Christie is even able to talk with Jared about her relationship with Ben.

For Christie right now, Ben is the man. They are different in a lot of ways, but none of the differences seem to cause them to clash. She can talk about anything with Ben, and he seems to know what she is going to say before she says it. He's not as sensitive as Jared, he's a little bossy, and he strikes her as a little arrogant at times, but nothing seems really out of place. He is smart, generous, and cute. He is happy to talk about God and spiritual things whenever she brings them up. She has even been able to talk with him about the big fight she had with Jared and how that relationship has been going.

So Christie—if she isn't kidding herself—has three soul matches. Two of them are possible marriage partners someday.

The potential marriage partner will enhance your spiritual life

If you're going to connect with someone as a marriage partner, you've got to have a person who will make your spiritual life go better, not worse.

What does this mean? You can talk easily about spiritual things, including questions and doubts, without feeling judged or lectured or put down. The two of you can pray out loud without it being weird or awkward or some big deal. You can read and discuss the Bible or solid books about God together and enjoy it.

This person makes you feel like you could be some kind of spiritual giant. And he or she never makes you feel spiritually small. "Never have a companion who casts you in the shade," said Baltasar Gracian. You want a marriage partner to bring you into the light, not cast you into the shade.

"Love does not dominate," said Goethe; "it cultivates." If you feel bullied rather than nourished, it's a good thing to have some doubts about another person.

As Christie thought through this critical point, she realized that she did have some questions about Ben. She felt better about her spiritual life when she was with Jared. She just felt more . . . spiritual. She and Abby had always been able to talk about God and life.

You will enhance his or her spiritual life

You want to make sure that you're as important to the other person's spiritual life as he or she is to yours.

Think about it. You aren't just spending time with some guy or girl. You have gotten into the world of a person who will be around *forever.* Even if you break up with him, you have been an actor on his stage. You've had an impact on him, for good or for bad. This complex, eternal, immortal being will be a different person because there was a *you,* and because you chose to be involved in his life.

So do you pray for her? Do you share things you've heard or read about God with her? Are you even hearing or reading these things about God so you can *be* an asset to her? Are you investing your time and energy and soul into making her a better person? Are you encouraging her life with God? Or are you frustrating and depressing and discouraging her and causing her to stumble in the dark?

There's no middle ground here. Either you are enhancing his spiritual life, or you are draining it. There is no neutral. If you have no strong drive to help him be fully what God designed him to be—even if that means he stays single or marries someone else—you are no where near having a good reason to get married.

This one scared Christie. Again, she had a genuine, mutual spiritual relationship with Abby. But even though she was more attracted to Ben than to Jared, she realized that very little of their time together had anything to do with God. With Jared, she saw that sometimes they spent more than half of their time on spiritual things. And it was so easy. It wasn't like they were trying to be superreligious people. She just found herself in a different frame of mind when she was with Jared.

You have interdependence

"In love," says the French proverb, "there is always one who kisses, and one who offers the cheek."

There is a mutual feel to great relationships. One of the best tests of a relationship that seems to be growing to something more serious is to see if it is *mutual*. You like each other at the same level, love each other at the same level, talk about the same amount of time, contact each other with about the same frequency, share about the same depth of problems or concerns.

It also means that there is no *dependence* in your relationship. Neither one of you feels immobilized if the other is not around or can't help. Neither of you has to wait for the other before you can make decisions. Neither of you has to ask permission before you feel like you can do something. This stuff isn't deep relationship; it's pathetic behavior and control. You want to have mutual *trust*, not dependent attachment of one of you on the other.

And it means that there is no *independence* in the relationship, either. Neither one of you feels like it's OK when you haven't spent any time together for weeks or longer. Neither of you makes decisions that affect the other—like where you're going to eat, what movie you'll attend, which people you'll invite along—without talking with the other. Neither of you does things and expects the other to automatically agree. This stuff isn't a freedom issue; it's common courtesy and decency. You want to have mutual *respect*, not independent lives that don't take the other into account.

What you want to have is *interdependence:* I need you and you need me, but not too much.

Christie and her friends—Abby, Jared, and Ben—all went to the same community college after graduating from high school. Her spiritual connection with Jared had continued to grow, but it seemed stagnated with Ben. At semester break, Christie broke off with Ben and started seeing Jared more frequently. She tried to keep up her friendship with Ben, but it became obvious very quickly that without the romantic dimension, he didn't put as much value as she did on the relationship. She also realized that he was hurt by her initiating the breakup, and she thought he would come around in time.

In February, Ben started dating Abby. That hurt a lot, but Christie had become even more sure that Ben was not the one for her. She couldn't help her feelings, though, and that did put a strain on her long relationship with Abby.

Love can be heard and absorbed both ways

As they got into their sophomore year, Christie and Jared realized that their relationship was something more than a friendship. The conversations got longer and deeper, the special moments came more frequently, and she felt the pull to be with Jared all the time. But as they neared the end of the school year, Christie started having some doubts.

Abby and Ben broke off their relationship quickly, and Abby and Christie now grew closer than ever as friends. "I don't know," Christie said to Abby. "I just don't know if Jared's the one."

"Are you crazy?" Abby asked in disbelief. "You've known each other forever, and you've been *very* serious for over a year. What's wrong?"

"I can't put my finger on it, exactly," Christie answered. "There are a lot of good things about our relationship. We really do care about each other, and he tries so hard. Only . . ."

"Only *what*?" Abby asked, furrowing her brow.

Christie closed her eyes briefly, and then looked straight into Abby's. "Only I can't feel it when he tries. I can't explain it, Abby, but the ways he tries to love me just don't connect with me at all."

Christie had been talking with the leader of one of the Christian groups on campus. He had told her about the key principle that marriages can't be great unless *love can be heard and absorbed both ways.* He told her that the way we show our love might not be the way another person can see love. He gave her some examples, in pairs:

Some People Show Their Love By:	Other People Feel Loved If We:
Giving advice	Listen
Listening	Give them advice
Spending time together	Know when to leave them alone
Giving the other space	Do everything together
Pointing out flaws or weak points	Compliment their strengths
Complimenting and encouraging	Point out their weak points
Helping the other stay busy	Slow them down
Calming the other down	Kick them in the pants
Giving gifts	Show them appreciation
Being grateful	Give them presents
Helping	Let them do it
Allowing others to try and fail	Bail them out
Doing what the other can't do	Show them how to do it
Teaching	Do it for them
Catering to the other's needs	Don't baby them
Trusting people to be responsible	Pamper them
Giving food or making meals	Help them watch their weight
Suggesting healthy eating or exercise	Buy them chocolate

When Christie went over the list, she realized that almost every thing Jared did to show his love was the opposite of what made Christie feel loved. And these weren't the things she felt she needed to become the kind of person she wanted to be.

Some of these differences can be made up by retraining ourselves. For example, we love to give advice to those we care about, but we force ourselves to shut up and listen to them talk at length about their problems instead. But this retraining is a very hard thing to do. It works against our personality, against who we are, and how we like to relate to other people. And it will be *very* hard to make this change stick for fifty or sixty years.

The truth is that we can love people in ways that don't make them feel loved. You've got to go over this list in detail to know if it is a *fit* both ways. And that means you have to know each other long enough that you can make sure she is not just adjusting her style of showing love *while you're dating.* Her efforts can be very deceptive, and the truth of a major-league love disconnect will come out after you're married.

It's not necessarily that he is being rotten or evil. He might just be trying to connect with you. But if it isn't really who he is, it is almost guaranteed to disappear after the honeymoon. You have to talk about this. You have to ask questions. And watch especially for the time when a nice thing he does annoys you. It doesn't matter if you need what he is offering; you will still resent it.

"What are you going to do?" Abby asked her longtime friend.

"It makes me sad to think about it," Christie said, tears forming in her eyes, "but I don't think he's the one for me." She was torn by many different feelings, including feeling like she had wasted so much time, but she knew that a few years was nothing compared to a lifetime.

And maybe Jared would still be her friend.

Your differences are complementary rather than destructive

And Jared remained Christie's friend. He and Abby and Christie were the "dynamic trio" as they finished junior college, and all three started at the nearby state university.

Christie went out with a number of guys, including two she met at a church about ten minutes from the campus. Dylan and

Bryan seemed like soul matches, just as Jared and Ben had. There was an outstanding spiritual connection with both of them. Dylan wanted to be a social worker, and Bryan wanted to be "the Christian Bill Gates" and change the world through business. There was real interdependence, and both of them loved Christie in a way that made her feel loved. As near as she could tell, they felt really cared about by her as well.

Dylan was very serious about everything, while Christie liked to be serious sometimes and to just relax and have fun sometimes. About the hundredth time she heard him say, "Christie, be serious," she thought she was going to scream. At the same time, his worrying about details and focus on punctuality had her telling him to "lighten up" just about as often. She didn't know that Dylan was telling one of his friends that he really liked her a lot, but he thought she might not be serious enough about making a difference in the world.

Christie wanted to like Dylan better because she thought she identified with his life goals, but she had to admit to Abby that Bryan's personality offset her weaknesses. Furthermore, her personality offset his weaknesses, without all of the tension and frustration and sense of being judged that seemed to hang over her relationship with Dylan.

People talk about having *complementary personalities,* or about one's strengths balancing the other's weaknesses, and how this is one of the best of reasons to get married. But you can't just say, "We love each other, and we have a lot of differences so we'll be able to help each other." In time, the differences are likely to annoy and frustrate and discourage you.

You have to make sure that the differences really are complementary and positive, and not just annoyingly different and negative. Watch for how you respond when he says or does something very different than what you would say or do in the same situation. If you say, "Now *that's* cool! I never thought of it (or did it) that way before," you're on the right track.

But if you say, "What on earth are you thinking? What made you say that? Why did you *do* that?" you are looking in the face of destructive difference. Make a run for it.

This person really is *the one*

It's possible that you might end up making it through all of the previous *best reasons* discussed in this chapter and still be thinking that this person might be *the one*. But you're smart enough to know how important this is, so you want some final checks, just like the astronauts go through before they blast into space.

That's what we've been trying to do together in this book. We've tried to make sure that you really understand this whole relationship aspect of your life, that you've spent a lot of time developing yourself, and that you spend just as much time observing the many people whom you get to know. And then, if you feel like a whole person who has found another whole person, you still want to make sure that you are thinking about marriage for the best of reasons, which is why we've walked together through this chapter.

Christie had walked this path with Ben, Jared, Dylan, and Bryan. Jared was still a great friend, and she was hoping that Dylan would be as well—although her experience with Ben had told her *maybe not*. She and Bryan were close, and their reasons for thinking about marriage seemed like the best. They were seniors in college now, and both of them were thinking about marriage. What should they do now?

Before they get any further, and certainly before they get engaged, they should make sure of some very important things (see chap. 9), because it will get harder to back out the longer they go on in "serious mode." They decide to ask the pastor at the church they are attending (the place where they met) to walk them through the "Twelve Things to Be Sure of Before You Get Married" before they consider getting engaged.

Christie is a little afraid because she thinks they might find something that will end her relationship with Bryan. But the more she thinks about it, the more she tells herself, *But if there is something, this is the time to find it out!*

Discussion Questions

On Your Own

- *Ask Your Parents:* Which of the reasons listed in this chapter were clear in your mind before you got married? Which ones were you least aware of or sure of? Could you give me some questions to ask my friend(s) to help us talk about these things? Could you point out details that I could look for to determine whether these things are present or not?
- *Ask Your Youth Pastor or Pastor:* Would you teach a class for our group on the *best* reasons to get married?

Together

- *Ask Yourselves:* (Take the time to write down a paragraph on why you think each of the *best reasons* applies to you. Then write down a paragraph on why you think each of the *best reasons* applies to the other person. Share your paragraphs with each other.) What concerns do I have about what the other person said? With what do I agree?
- *Ask Each Other:* What do you think of the paragraphs I wrote? Why? How do they compare with the paragraphs you wrote? What are the reasons for the differences? Do the *best reasons* really apply to us? Why or why not?
- *Ask Your Youth Pastor or Pastor:* Would you tell us whether you think we are considering marriage for the *best reasons* listed in this chapter? Would you tell us where you think our reasons might *not* be the best?

*It destroys one's nerves to be amiable every day
to the same human being.*
British Prime Minister Benjamin Disraeli

twelve things
to be sure of before
you get married
chapter 9

How important is it to be sure, very sure? Even after you've
known someone for a while and you've satisfied yourself that
you're both ready and have great reasons to get married?

Well, this is it. It's the whole ball game. If you make an average
choice in this relationship, it will to be hard to have an outstanding life. This person might be decent and intelligent and caring, but
if he's not the best one for you, it will slowly take you down, peg
by peg by peg. If you make a bad choice, you will have to fight every
day the rest of your life not to hate him.

You can be so sure and still be wrong. Almost everyone who
goes *into* marriage is sure—sure that this is as good as life and love
can get, sure that this will be
great at least most of the
time, sure that this will give
her what her heart is longing
for. But half or more of the

> *Mourning the loss of someone we
> love is happiness compared with
> having to live with someone we hate.*
> **Bruyère**

people who are *sure* will end up divorced. Many of the rest will be hampered in their race for God and His kingdom.

This person looks great, even wonderful. But you're going to meet hundreds or thousands of people of the opposite sex in the next twenty-five years. Will this person match up well with *all* of them? Beyond that, will he or she look like a *better choice* than all of them?

You might think so right now, while you're sailing above the earth on cloud 9. But what about later? You might meet someone who is so fabulous that you can't even believe God turned your desires into a person—but when you're married, your spouse might only seem half as good. You will be basically out of options—but you will still feel it, and it will hurt, and you will feel that sense of *I missed it* for the rest of your life. Or perhaps you will dump your first mate and really derail yourself with God.

Am I saying that you should wait forever? That you should never get married, because someone better could always come along? No. Absolutely not. That would be missing the point by a hundred miles. What I am saying is that you *must be absolutely sure*. Beyond a reasonable doubt. Beyond an *unreasonable* doubt. Beyond any current rush of emotion. Beyond any romantic notions, or hormonal surges, or passionate desires.

Beyond everything except this: *I know, I am sure, that this really is as good as it could possibly get.*

It's worth taking the time to be that sure.

How Sure Is Sure?

Even if the other person is a Christian and claims to love you, that may not be enough to ensure a happy marriage. His Christianity may be a sham (see Matthew 7:16–20), or what he calls "love" might really be a desperate need, as we've discussed earlier.

But it might not be a problem just with another person. There are situations we can be in at certain points in our lives that can make a decision look right and great—but after the smoke clears it looks a lot different. Our feelings were based on things that were real, but they were exaggerated for some reason.

We should be very careful not to move ahead into marriage when our lives are involved with any of the following situations.

Situation #1: Your emotions are at an extreme pitch. If you're in the midst of a turbulent time, a time of great passion and enthusiasm or great loneliness and depression, it's probably time to let your head investigate your heart.

Cassandra was acting in her last play in her senior year. She could feel the sadness and tears bubbling up and over at every practice. Everything made her cry, and she wanted to hug her friends every time she saw them. Her heightened sensitivity was due to her feeling that her life was about to change in some dramatic ways. It would have been easy for her to latch onto one of her male friends right then. She thought this would give her some kind of anchor against the waves of change. Bad plan.

Situation #2: You're in the midst of great change. When your life is going through great change, when you're in the middle of a big transition (like changing from one school to another, changing your course of study, moving to a new area), the need for a strong relationship to anchor you is obvious. You've got a good chance, though, of throwing your anchor into acid. Great decisions are seldom made when our lives and hearts are up in the air.

Situation #3: You've just had a significant failure. Nick and Katy had been close for two years. They had experienced so much fun together. And then both of them got hit with failure at the same time. Nick had been a point guard on the basketball team, the leader of the team, the player who always took the last shot to win the game. And in the state championship game three days before, he had missed not one but *two* easy shots in the last thirty seconds to cost his team the game. Two days later, Katy failed to make the premier choir after taking extensive voice lessons and practicing nonstop for six months.

They threw themselves into each other's arms, cried together, comforted each other. OK so far. But this is a very bad time to make a commitment. They will look like each other's best (and maybe only) friend, but turning that comforter into a life partner could be the worst kind of mistake. This current comfort and understanding might not be the answer to the big question of love.

Situation #4: You've been hurt. After you've been wounded by another person, the best medication may seem to be another relationship. The cavalry has arrived! You're saved! You might not throw out the baby with the bath water, but you can throw out your common sense for the opportunity of being rescued. The best thing you can do is to appreciate the hurt—to ask God what this can teach you, and how this can make you better at relationships in the future. It's all right to get help from another person. Just make sure this relationship doesn't get out of control or get too serious at this time.

Situation #5: You're wrestling with God about your relationship with Him. If we're going to have an authentic life, sooner or later we're going to have to wrestle with God. Probably several times. A human relationship can seem almost like a relief during these times. It can seem almost easy and natural compared with this complex relationship with an invisible being. But a human relationship during such a time of struggle may distract us from our business with God, and will probably end up giving us a bad relationship with the person at the same time.

If we're facing any of these emotional situations, we should stop before even getting to the "Twelve Things to Be Sure of Before You Get Married." Our evaluators aren't functioning properly. We won't be able to do an honest job on the list of twelve. So go back through the list above, and honestly ask yourself if you are facing any of these situations.

It's OK to be in a struggle. It's OK to be there for a while. But it's not OK to make a rest-of-your-life decision while you're there. You're a whole lot smarter than that.

The Twelve Last Checkpoints

Perhaps the other person really is a Christian and has overcome any marriage-destroying problems from his or her past. Maybe you're sure you're not in one of the situations described above. But that still might not be enough to ensure the true oneness of spirit that God designed marriage to be. In order to have this oneness, we need to be sure of at least twelve things.

1. You are aware of and can survive the transitions of life and love.

Life is full of change and phases and passages. Do you know what they are? For example, did you know that you are likely to consider working in at least three different careers over the course of your life? And that your spouse is likely to do the same?

How are you and this other person handling the small changes you have already faced? If you're already struggling with changes, even if everything else looks positive, you could be in serious trouble.

The only constants in life are God and change. If you're surviving the small changes, that's not good enough. If you're thriving when these changes come, that's better—but this might still not be a sure test of your flexibility and adaptability. It's only when you are able to make the change work for your relationship—only when you are able to take advantage of this change to make your relationship even better—that you can really be sure that you've struck gold.

2. Both of you are ready to give up some of your "freedom."

A marriage comes with duties and obligations, boundaries and restraints. Have the two of you talked about them? Have you been honest about your expectations and points of resistance?

Right now, you can decide to go where you want, when you want, with whom you want. A married person has to involve the other person in most of those decisions, if for no other reason than to make the marriage and the family schedule work. Will you be ready to do that? Will you be willing to explain what you're doing and why? Or will you feel like you have a big brother or big sister looking over your shoulder and making you follow orders. You may have to give up some freedom, but you don't want to give up your individuality. Losing freedom of movement is one thing; losing freedom of soul is a lot more serious.

A lot of people talk about the value of having someone to hold you "accountable." There can be some value in this, if we don't give that person too much power and we don't let him or her become a poor substitute for the Holy Spirit. But even if you think it might be valuable, are you sure you won't hate it? Human beings are not designed to be captives (see Galatians 5:1–13). Will you end up fighting against the expectations and restraints for the rest of your life?

3. The two of you have a truly intimate one-spirit friendship (soul mates).

Perhaps you and your friend like your time together. There aren't core annoyances and frustrations. Does life make more sense after you've talked it out? If it does, that's a good sign. This relationship needs to be a best friendship before it can possibly be a best marriage.

Just being attracted to each other won't be enough. Even being passionate about each other won't be enough. You need to know that if this other person is the soup, you're the sandwich.

You've got to know that you're different, but that together you make a whole new unity. If you're the same, that's bad. If you're different and don't match up, that's bad. It's only when your difference adds up to something unified and solid and whole that you can be sure.

4. The other person is wise, and not just a "Christian."

If you're a Christian, of course you want your potential mate to be a Christian. What you believe about God and eternity is the core of who you are and will be as a human being. If you believe God is the center, and she doesn't even think God *exists*—or that God is who He says He *is*—you've got a gap that makes the Grand Canyon look like a gopher hole.

But just being a Christian isn't enough. There are plenty of miserable Christians, discouraging Christians, and nasty Christians. There are Christians who will see Christianity much differently than you do. These conflicting views of life and God could cause major marital conflicts. What evidence is there of the seven-pillar wisdom of James 3:17 that we discussed in chapter 3, "Recognizing a Person Worth Knowing and Marrying"? Your mate won't have those things without a deep relationship with God.

And this should go deeper than just talking a good game. He should *live* a good game. And that starts with how he treats you in the everyday dance of life. Nothing is easier than for a person to make people *outside* the marriage and family think he's great while he's making those *inside* totally miserable. The words of the German proverb are chilling: "Street angel, house devil."

5. You are able to love each other and meet each other's needs.

Have you been honest about those needs? Or have you held back, embarrassed? She can't meet your needs if she doesn't know what they are. If she really knew what they were, would her interest in you still be the same? Or might she think the price is a little too high?

You also have to have a brutally realistic assessment of his needs and expectations. Are you going to be willing to listen, every night, over and over, to the details of his crummy work situation? Are you going to be willing to drop what you're doing to help him with a project after he's overcommitted himself *again*?

And both of you have to be sure that you're free of the relationship-crushing expectation that you will meet all of the other's needs. This other person isn't God, or the rest of the human race, or even the only friend of the opposite sex whom you will ever need.

6. Both of you have self-control.

A lack of self-control on the part of either of you now will not get better after you're married. How you handle time alone together is an important test. Are you building each other up and protecting each other's souls, or do you find yourself pushing the boundaries and feeling like you're failing?

And how do you handle disagreements? Is there a lot of anger? Are things said that hurt deeply, and are hard to forget even after you forgive? You'll need to see a lot of patience now, in the face of stupid and upsetting things, to be sure that you can make it when you face a *lifetime* of stupid and upsetting things. "It takes patience to appreciate domestic bliss," said George Santayana; "volatile spirits prefer unhappiness."

The Bible tells us that we should "be sober! Be on the alert! Your adversary the Devil is prowling around like a roaring lion, looking for anyone he can devour" (1 Peter 5:8).

7. You have developed a strategy to avoid the daily irritations of life.

In many ways, marriage makes life harder. Daily life can take its toll. Have both of you faced up to this? Do you acknowledge the destructive potential of daily life? "Love is an ideal thing, marriage a real thing," said Goethe; "a confusion of the real with the ideal never goes unpunished." Thinking that marriage will be like dating, courtship, engagement, and romance is probably a contender for dumbest thought of the year.

How well do the two of you do, the more you spend time together? Do you feel like you need some time away? That it's all just too much, and you're getting stuck in the details? Imagine how that feeling will expand when you're bouncing off each other every day for fifty years! Small annoyances now will seem like reasons to declare war after you've seen him or her five thousand times.

"The most fatal disease of friendship is gradual decay," said Dr. Johnson, "or dislike hourly increased by causes too slender for complaint, and too numerous for approval." This decay will be like a malignant cancer. Are you sure the beginnings of the disease aren't already present?

8. You could postpone the wedding date for five years and still marry each other.

If one of you is eager to move ahead because you think the other person might have a change of heart, you've got pretty strong proof that this relationship isn't as strong as it appears to be.

If you don't feel that you can wait, why not? Is it desperation? Lust? Fear? Are you afraid that you'll fall apart if you don't seal this up in a tight vow or covenant? Do you feel that you'd better strike while the iron is hot—because the iron might cool off? If so, you should know that *these are reasons to wait, not to move ahead.* They're the opposite of what they seem to be. In marriage, speed is never your friend.

9. The two of you have similar views on bearing and raising children.

Children are blessings that come with major challenges and problems. Researchers say that two-thirds of couples experience a sharp drop in marital satisfaction after the birth of a first child. Do you have any idea what the other person really thinks and feels about this major undertaking?

If you're thinking *kids are the greatest thing ever,* and he's thinking *I guess having kids is OK,* you can't even imagine how far apart you are in your thinking!

You don't have to have kids if you marry. And you don't have to have any certain number of kids. But you'd better know that both of you see eye-to-eye on this one. Some people stay in unhappy marriages because of the children—but a lot of people are *in* unhappy marriages *because of the children.*

Children will change your relationship—are *guaranteed* to change your relationship—in a thousand different ways. Explore those scenarios in a thousand different conversations with each other.

10. Neither of us will enter the marriage with thoughts that it might not work.

How deep is the commitment? Is it proven? Does he or she have a healthy number of long-term relationships?

In a day of high divorce, "trial" marriages, and living together, marriage can seem a whole lot less permanent than it used to. But going into marriage with the idea that it might not work is *guaranteed to make it more likely that it won't.*

The explorer Hernando Cortez, when faced with the possibility that his crews might turn back to the ships if the going got tough, *burned the ships.* If you want to be sure that both of you will work to make this marriage a success, you've got to burn the ships as well. No turning back. If either of you thinks there are any ships still in the harbor, you're not ready to get married.

11. Both of you have done an in-depth study of marriages.

Have you looked closely at the marriages of your parents and her parents and of other people who have influenced both of you? Have you looked especially closely at those that are troubled or have failed? If you're saying, "I don't think she will turn out like her mother," or "I'm sure glad he's not like his father," you're probably taking up residence in la-la land.

And are you facing up to reality and the scary similarities to your own relationship? Have you talked deeply about how to overcome these problems—or are you both avoiding the problems and acting like they don't exist?

12. Both of you have each lived long enough and experienced enough and grown enough to make a wise decision.

Do you really know that experience—life experience—is your friend? That the longer you think about a decision, the more viewpoints from which you observe and evaluate it, the more likely that it will be a good one?

People change attitudes and desires and careers and jobs and all sorts of other life components. Are you going to be a casualty of normal growth and change? Are you going to find yourself saying, "Wow! I sure didn't see that! Where did he come up with *that*?"

Even if you wait until you're thirty to get married, if you both live until you're ninety that gives you *sixty years* to be married. That's plenty of time to enjoy a beautiful marriage.

And way too much time to hate an ugly relationship.

"To cheat oneself out of love," said the writer Soren Kierkegaard, "is the greatest deception of which there is no reparation in either time or eternity."

One of the surest ways to cheat yourself out of love is to miss one of the twelve things to be sure of before you get married.

Bon Voyage

How you go into marriage (from a +10 to a −10) determines the path that is going to bear either good or bad fruit ten, twenty, or thirty years from now. You really, really want to be sure.

As counselor and author Dan Allender has written, "I want to know I am making the 'right' choice. . . . I have ways of making assessments. I can see how she handles conflict, loneliness, shame, loss, feedback, my sin, disappointment. I can observe how she relates to a broad range of people and situations. I can interact with her heart and assess whether I want to muddle through life with her."[1]

As we read about Christie's determination in the last chapter, we could see that she wanted to make sure she was heading into more than just a good marriage. She knew that she and Bryan were moving in that direction for the best of reasons. She insisted that they take at least six more months to make sure of the twelve important things discussed in this chapter.

They found that they had major unresolved questions on four of these twelve things:

Bryan was a little shaky on the "freedom" question (#2); Christie was seriously annoyed by a number of Bryan's habits and routines (#7); they had views on children that were *very* far apart (#9); and they hadn't really looked closely at other marriages to see what they could learn (#11).

They spent those six months and were satisfied with what they'd learned and done, except for the question about children. After four more months, they had a hard-earned agreement that seemed right and good to both of them.

Christie and Bryan had made it so far. Now for the last step. Was Bryan really *the one*? Her pastor told her there were ten secrets of knowing you'd found "The Right One."

Discussion Questions

On Your Own

- *Ask Your Parents:* Would you go through these twelve things and tell me how many of them you were really sure of before you got married? On the ones you weren't sure about, how did they affect your marriage?

- *Ask Your Youth Pastor or Pastor:* With what you see going on in my life right now, do you think I am in a turbulent time that could affect my judgment about relationships? Is there anyone I should keep at a distance? Why?

Together

- *Ask Yourselves:* Go through the list on your own and rate your certainty on each item on a one-to-ten scale. Then, write a short paragraph on each, explaining why you rated it as you did.

- *Ask Each Other:* Discuss your ratings and short paragraphs. Commit to taking as much time as necessary to thoroughly go through these twelve things together. Discuss whether you would be willing to study one a month for the next twelve months. Begin now with number one.

True love is like seeing ghosts:
We all talk about it, but few of us have ever seen one.
La Rochefoucauld

ten ways to know you've found "the one"

chapter 10

This is your final gut-check before you commit your life, with no turning back, to a relationship. Read it now. And then read it again before you do the ring thing or the vow thing.

Ten Assurances That You Can Have for Life

This chapter is a gut-check, but it's also about the mountain-top. We want to finish the "match" section of this book on a high note: What is the best you can have? What will this really be like and feel like? What will you need to know beforehand—*beforehand*, since you won't be able to choose another path. You don't want to say, in ten or twenty years, *I wish I had known then what I know now.*

So we're going to be bold. Take some time to review this checklist when you think you've found a special person. Don't do it just to avoid a mistake. Do it because you want to "shoot for the

Anything will give up its secrets if you love it enough.
George Washington Carver

moon." Don't settle for anything else. Don't rest until you're sure you've found *the one.*

Here are the *ten ways to know for sure.*

1. God seems more real to both of you.

God seems more alive during your times together and your conversations. Your relationship causes you both to grow in "knowledge and every kind of discernment" (Philippians 1:9). You build each other's relationship with God. You expand each other's thoughts about Him. When he talks about his experience with God, his ideas and impressions about Him *connect* with your spirit in a way that makes you know that God is speaking to you through this other human being. Those ideas make spiritual and practical *sense.*

"Love," said the French writer Proust, "is space and time made directly perceptible to the heart." In a way, love is *God* made directly perceptible to the heart (which shouldn't be surprising since "God *is* love"; 1 John 4:16b). Make sure her passion for God doesn't fizzle. What happens to her passion for Him over time? If it fizzles for her, it's guaranteed that it will be harder for you to keep your passion for God alive.

2. You're both free to be who you are.

You are able to be deeply honest with each other. You can let the other see who you really are. Together you can rejoice "in the truth" (1 Corinthians 13:6). Both of you are able to be genuine and authentic (see Romans 12:9).

You find that you are hypersensitive, but it's about the other person's feelings rather than your own. You want him to have no barriers to free expression with you. And you want to—need to— make yourself known, even down to the warts and pimples of who you are. It's OK, because he makes you *know* that it's OK.

3. You contribute to each other's growth.

You truly are intimate, one-spirit friends. You sharpen each other (see Proverbs 27:17). Sparks fly, but something better results from the friction. You always trust (see 1 Corinthians 13:7) that the other person is going to say things and push things because she really is the best for you. You constantly stretch each other and push each other to take risks—and she can move out of her comfort zone because she is secure in her relationship with you. You help each other solve problems.

You define friendship the same way. You support each other's interests and other relationships—including other opposite-sex friends. Both of you believe you can be much greater if you live life together, and you have many details and examples to support this belief. You know that he is in it for *you,* and not just his own agenda.

4. You're sold out on each other's success.

There are no doubts about the question, Is she in it for me? She listens to, encourages, and expands your dreams. Being with her makes you feel like a bigger and better person. She affirms you rather than tears you down. She celebrates rather than criticizes your development and achievement. She wants you to be all you can be, and she can see your potential. She can see things about you that you can't even see. Through it all, she "bears all things" (1 Corinthians 13:7). She protects you, your environment (so you can do what you were put here to do), and your sense of self-worth from relatives and friends and strangers.

"Love does not consist in gazing at each other," said writer and aviator Saint-Exupéry, "but in looking together in the same direction." And you find yourselves consistently looking in the same direction. This means that other people are viewed as assets to the other rather than competitors.

5. You can't escape equality.

Both of you submit to each other "out of reverence for Christ" and "as to the Lord" (Ephesians 5:21–22 NIV). Neither of you is hung up about being "in charge." You both take equal responsibility for resolving problems and disagreements. You fix the problem rather than fixing the blame. You have fifty-fifty conversations; there is no "I just want to listen." Neither of you is a clam, open now but ready to snap shut later. You both share deeply original and genuine information with each other.

You share a mutual, tested willingness to give up desires and to sacrifice. And you have agreed on a split of responsibilities, an equal valuing of those duties, and a method for redefining these activities in the future. Both of you play equal roles when socializing or ministering, with neither of you either taking away the other's place or dumping your own on him or her.

6. The packaging is in perspective.

You're connected to the being, the soul, inside, not just to the packaging—the way he looks and seems outside. You like him even when he is grungy. You're proud of who he is and how he looks, but not in a way that makes you "show him off" to others so you can feel good about yourself.

If she were *disfigured,* you would still love her. Even when you picture her as an elderly person, you're still nuts about her. Take time to really picture these possibilities. Make *sure* you know what your response would be.

7. The "I can't believe it" factor dominates.

He is a lot more than you think you deserve. He is exceedingly above anything you could ask for or imagine (see Ephesians 3:20). You have an undeniable sense that you've *always* known him. The feelings aren't manufactured or forced; the feelings are just *there.*

She stands up well to a large frame of reference (you've known many people of the opposite sex, so you know what you're talking about). Even the best of those you knew before seem like only previews. And, in a reasonable way, she lives up to your ideals.

8. Contentment is as strong as desire.

You didn't seek a mate; he sneaked up on you while you were out and about, learning to live and enjoying God's work. The relationship has been given the test of time—time to see his character, time to see through any fatal flaws.

There is no manipulation or pressure in the relationship. You're incredibly happy with your friendship. You're committed to the best path for your love, even if that means you should wait years before you marry. Like Jacob, you know that your Rachel is worth waiting for, and working for, for many years.[1] The joy is now, in the midst of your great friendship, not "after we get married."

9. He or she doesn't fizzle under failure.

You have strong finishes together during tests, obstacles, and crises. You've passed the inevitable tests brought from outside your relationship—from people and situations. Failure and mistakes draw you closer. Problems present opportunity, not annoyance.

She loves you at your worst, and is kind even when you disagree. Tension and stress don't produce ugly interactions. You don't have wars, either hot (rage, anger) or cold (silence, looks). What if you can say, "but we've never had any of these challenges"? You're probably years away from being ready to marry.

10. His or her seriousness is matched by playfulness.

You can relax and really let your guard down. There is the joy and freedom that comes from innocence and purity. There is healthy teasing that stays within bounds. There is comfort and peace in physical closeness. You sense that playfulness will be one of the main ingredients for wiping out sexual fears, sexual negotiation, and sexual games after you're married.

You can laugh at life. You can laugh at each other without hurting each other's feelings—and you're really *sure* of that. And you can laugh at yourselves. You make self-deprecating comments without the other thinking you're a loser, or without you doing it so you can get him to praise you. You can just *play*.

If both of you give a hearty and solid *Yes!* to every point on this list—after addressing all the earlier steps covered in this book—you've found a possible lifelong partner. Both of you have found a soul match. You've found *the one*.

In a recent poll of never-married people in their twenties, 94 percent said that "the first requirement in a spouse is being a soul mate." A total of 87 percent said they will find that person when "they are ready." And yet, in the same poll, "More than two-thirds (68 percent) said a good marriage is tougher to achieve today than in their parents' generation. Half (52 percent) said they see so few happy marriages that they question it as a way of life."[2]

So there you have the conflict. We want to find *the one*—our soul mate, our soul match. We have an idealistic and romantic notion that we will indeed find him or her. But when we look at the reality of marriage, we know that it's tough—tougher now than ever. We haven't even *seen* very many happy marriages, to give us either guidance or encouragement. We know that half of all marriages will end in divorce and many others in despair. And yet, most of those people went into marriage believing they had found *the one*.

You're going to beat the odds. You believe your having a soul match is crucial if you're going to get married, and you believe you're going to wait until that person comes along. There's good news.

You can.

The Best for Both

These tips aren't just for you to marry well. They're for the other person to marry well, too. *Both* of you have to know that these secrets are yours. If one of you is sure and the other isn't, you still don't have a match.

It has to be the best relationship for *both* of you. This is much more of a test than having just one person satisfied.

Take the time to make sure you're both on board. And try hard not to pressure the other into agreeing that all ten are in place. "We all have to make decisions on the basis of limited data," said Peter L. Bernstein. "[But] courtship with a future spouse is shorter than the lifetime that lies ahead."

Take your time. You're going for checking off these ten tips times two people.

And this is where Christie and Bryan, now twenty-three, decided that they had a roadblock to moving ahead. Bryan told her, and their pastor, that he was sure all ten were in place for him. Christie had some doubts about that, doubts that kept growing the longer she thought about them.

And she had doubts of her own. She felt like several of the secrets pointed to missing pieces in their relationship. And she knew that they weren't pieces that they could or should try to manufacture.

With pain far greater than her earlier relationships, she decided to stop their path to the altar. In a tear-filled, emotional, and—at times—intense session with their pastor, she expressed her doubts. Ironically, they were doubts that made her certain. Certain that Bryan was *not the one.*

They kept up their friendship for almost a year, but Christie knew that Bryan was heartbroken and that they would need time and probably some separation before they could hope to restore their friendship.

And five years later, after a second pass through the ten secrets, Christie married him. But the "him" wasn't Bryan. It was Jeffrey. He was clearly and truly *the one*. And Christie finally got rewarded for her patience and wisdom.

The absolute love of a lifetime.

Discussion Questions

On Your Own

- *Ask Your Parents:* At what point in your relationship did each of you come to the conclusion that you had found "The Right One"? How long did it take for you to reach this point in your relationship? Did each of you realize this at different times or at the same time?

- *Ask Your Youth Pastor or Pastor:* Please read over these "Ten Ways to Know You've Found *the One.*" Do you have anymore information to add to these ten clues? How would you rate these ten ways against one another in terms of importance? Is it possible to remain open-eyed and rational about these criteria in the heat of an emotional relationship?

Together

- *Ask Each Other:* (Make sure you are familiar with the "Ten Ways to Know You've Found *the One.*") Why do you think we are right for each other? (Listen closely as the other person answers this question. Then compare your responses to these "Ten Ways" and see how similar or different they are.) What insights have we discovered together? How will this affect our relationship?

Life
Right Now
Part 4

I want you to be without concerns. An unmarried man is concerned about the things of the Lord—how he may please the Lord. . . . An unmarried woman . . . is concerned about the things of the Lord, so that she may be holy both in body and in spirit.
1 Corinthians 7:32–34

celebrating singleness
chapter 11

Kaylee hadn't seen McKenzie for almost three years, ever since their graduation party after high school. McKenzie's voice mail message had been a great surprise: "I'm coming into town for the weekend. Let's do lunch!"

They had greeted each other with enthusiastic hugs in the lobby of the little Italian café across from the campus. But the lunch had quickly become depressing for Kaylee.

"You won't believe what's happened!" McKenzie spurted even before they had gotten into their seats.

"Tell me!" Kaylee said as she scooted into the booth.

"I'm going to be married!"

"Wow! That's great," Kaylee said. "Tell me about him."

"You *know* him, Kaylee. It's Paul!"

Kaylee felt queezy. She and Paul had dated seriously for all

We must creatively develop a theology of marriage and singleness that grapples honestly with the challenging but unambiguous message in the New Testament that sometimes marriage, and not singleness, may be the lesser of two options.[1]
Lauren F. Winner

of their junior year and most of their senior year in high school. The breakup had been sort of both of their ideas. But now, hearing that her old friend from middle school days was going to marry him, she felt . . . empty. "That's great!" she said, lying.

After a few minutes of updating on the engagement, McKenzie dropped the other shoe. "What about you?"

"What do you mean?"

"Have you found your Mr. Right yet?"

I'm not even looking, Kaylee thought. "Not yet," she replied.

"That's too bad," McKenzie said, sympathetically. "But don't give up hope. I know there's a great guy out there who's just right for you."

Until that moment, Kaylee hadn't felt sorry for herself. And she hadn't given up hope, because she didn't even know she had hopes to give up.

I've got to get serious about finding someone, she told herself.

The Problem of Singleness

Most of you reading these words are probably single. And for many of you, sooner or later, your singleness will seem like a problem.

But it isn't.

Why not? Because that's how God made you. In fact, singleness can't be too bad an option *because God starts everyone out that way.*

We don't have to give in to feelings of getting left behind, like Kaylee is about to do. Or feelings of desperation, which Kaylee will have if she focuses on her "problem" for too long. Why not? Why can we avoid giving in to these feelings? Because singleness is not a defective condition.

Much of life is designed to make you feel that singleness *is* a defective condition. When you are a young person, life can ask you questions like, "Why don't you have a special person in your life? What's the matter with you? Are you some kind of loser?" As you get older, life can ask you other things, like, "Still single, heh?

I guess you just haven't found the right person yet? What are you doing to meet Mr. (or Miss) Right?" The way people look at you can also change as you get older—especially after *they've* gotten married.

The church generally hasn't done any better. Often, it acts like singleness is a problem in need of a solution. In many ways, it pushes marriage as the mountaintop of relationship (the "holy state of matrimony") even more than many people outside the church do. It's partly because the church sees itself as the great defender of marriage. That's not a bad role for the church, as long as it doesn't become the great defender of the idea of marriage as the best way for everyone.

Why would it become that?

Partly, it's because the church at times misses the bigger point about marriage and family. What's that? That there is a *family of God*. Ultimately, it's the only family that has *must* written all over it. If you're not in that family, you're really out in the cold. If you have a nice family on earth but you aren't part of the ultimate family in heaven, you are in reality an orphan. At the end of life, there is only one family. The family you should plan to join isn't hers or his. It's *His*.

In too many churches, people are split into "singles" and "marrieds," and further subdivided (young singles, older singles, etc.), and the split defines people's relationship to the church. This is a tragedy, because we're all part of the same family.

And in too many churches, singles groups are actually singles bars for Christians (where we don't have alcohol but do have wolves), where people can meet someone to marry and get rid of their singleness. Many of these groups exist more to provide chances to meet potential partners than to maximize the joy of the single life.

Another reason the church can overpush marriage is that it can take Ephesians 5:21–33 way too far.[2] Instead of seeing this passage for what Paul himself says it is, an *illustration*—"This mystery is profound, but I am talking about *Christ and the church"* (v. 32, emphasis added)—it makes marriage the pinnacle of life because it puts us in a relationship that is somehow like Christ's relationship with the church. (Unfortunately, some men have carried this illustration too far and started thinking of themselves as the god of the marriage).

God uses many illustrations in the Bible. For example, we are the sheep and He is the shepherd (see John chap. 10). But this doesn't mean that being member of a "flock" (church member) where we have a "shepherd" (pastor) is the highest form of relationship. And it's not the highest, *even though this is also a picture of Christ and the church.*

A third reason for the marriage push is that to many people in the church, singleness looks like an unstable condition. "He'll settle down after he gets married." "She'll be less anxious about her life when she finds the right guy." It's like singleness is the disease and marriage is the cure. But divorce and separation claim the opposite: they say that *marriage* is the disease and *singleness* is the cure. Others who stay in miserable marriages for various reasons can also feel that marriage is the disease.

Which opinion is right? Is singleness the disease, or is it marriage?

Neither. Marriage is certainly not a disease, although being in the wrong marriage can turn your life into a long bout of relational cancer. But singleness is also most certainly not a disease—*unless you think it is.* You're the only one who can turn your singleness into a disease, by treating it like there's something wrong with it.

Instead of acting like the world is your oyster and celebrating your singleness, you can believe that you've got a bad case of relational flu. Maybe relational pneumonia. Maybe even relational cancer.

But you would be creating the problem in your own head. Singleness is a gift. It's not a gift in the sense that some people use the phrase ("she has the gift of singleness," whatever that means). Singleness is a gift because God gives it to everyone. No one starts out married. And singleness is a gift because it provides the time to think and do things without the encumbrances of marriage. It gives the time to "be devoted to the Lord without distraction" (1 Corinthians 7:35).

So both singleness and marriage can be wonderful conditions. Neither in itself is a disease, although we can turn either of them ugly. But if you're going to make a biblical case for which one is better for most people (it's not required that you make this case, but it *is* interesting), it would probably be *singleness*. Read 1 Corinthians 7 for yourself and see what you think.

In fact, it's even more dramatic than that. If you went through the chapter, did you see it? Paul seems to be saying that singleness is the preferred state. Look at verse 29: "The time is limited, so from now on those who have wives *should live as though they had none*" (1 Corinthians 7:29; emphasis added). Married people, in other words, should "live single."

Paul is not, of course, saying that you should ignore your spouse if you're married. He's simply saying that you'd better focus on God and His kingdom (see Matthew 6:33) and the race you're supposed to be running[3] before you focus on your spouse or anything else. He's proposing a radical idea: married single person. Paul is saying that you need to be single-minded in your devotion to God for the rest of your life—even if you happen to be married.

When a married person says something like, "I'd really like to do that, but I can't do anything unless my spouse agrees" or "I never do anything unless my spouse is with me 100 percent," you're hearing the death of singleness in a marriage. This is letting a spouse take God's place. This person is losing her identity. This person is letting another human being determine her destiny rather than letting God guide her.

Your relationship with God, your *single*-minded devotion to God, should be the centerpiece of your life. Your relationship with God, not a marriage, should be the defining point of your being. Kyleen is a whole person, even though she broke up with Paul, even though she isn't seeing anyone special, even though marriage isn't even on her mind, even though she's being swamped by bad feelings.

Singleness, whether you're single or married, is the real deal. It's worth understanding this, and it's worth celebrating this. We even have a model for this. Who is that? Well, the greatest person who ever lived was Christ, and He was single. He is the real deal. He wasn't incomplete or unstable or relationally sick.

So if you really want to be like Christ, you'll live the single life—whether you're single or married.

Some Important Questions

I want you to have some answers to some key singleness questions. Thinking through these issues well will help you live a contented, full single life.

Let's look in depth at each of these questions.

What am I supposed to do with my singleness?

Nothing.

That's right. Nothing. We're not supposed to do anything with our singleness. It's the way God made us. It doesn't need to be fixed because it isn't broken.

Singleness is a complete condition all by itself. And marriage is *not* the destination of singleness. Marriage is just one of the choices that a single person has. Singleness, like marriage, is a whole way to live. One isn't better than the other.

And marriage isn't the epitome, the ultimate, the highest. God is.

Is singleness a time of preparation, or is it a time of abundance? Or is it both?

Singleness is both. It is first a time of preparation.

But the question is, "Preparation for *what*?"

Singleness is a time to prepare for *life*, not for marriage. It's a time to develop yourself and test yourself and enjoy yourself. It's a time to learn and serve and grow. The whole world is out there, waiting for you, and you're probably just what it needs.

Singleness is a time to prepare yourself to be whole. You shouldn't waste your time trying to find your "other half." If there's only half of you, you'd better find the other half *before* you consider getting married, not after.

You're not automatically incomplete if you're not married. Was Jesus incomplete? No. And you can be married and still be incomplete. Or worse. Real incompleteness results from a marriage that leaves us empty. Singleness doesn't limit love, and marriage doesn't guarantee happiness.

You don't want to save yourself for marriage. You want to save yourself for *God*.

Even if part of the time of preparation is to become a person worthy of knowing and marrying, it should be a *thorough* time. If you wanted to be an accountant or engineer or teacher, you would have to spend at least four years preparing. To be really good, you might have to spend even more time. Know what? Being married is a *whole* lot harder than being an accountant or engineer or teacher.

And singleness is, second, a time of abundance.

"I have come that they may have life and have it in abundance" (John 10:10), said Jesus. If you have a relationship with God through Christ, you don't have to wait to have a full life. You've already *got* a full life. That's why He came—so you could have that kind of life.

Don't trade a full life for a miserable life. Don't give it up unless you're sure beyond a reasonable doubt. You might think, "I can't cancel the wedding if the guests have been invited and we've rented the tuxedos!" Sure you can. In some cases, the wedding might be the perfect tool to bring the nagging questions and doubts to the surface. Don't be pressured into giving up your abundant life because the wedding guests are arriving. They can have lunch and go home and watch television. You'll have to live with the day forever.

Only yield your life of abundance if you can live it just as abundantly as a married single person.

Are there any reasons to stay single?

Marriage is not the reasonable conclusion to your singleness. In fact, there are some important arguments for singleness as a reasonable conclusion to your singleness. There are at least seven reasons to stay single.

Reason #1: Freedom. We can serve God with our whole hearts (see 1 Corinthians 7:32–34). When we're single, we're not tempted to divide our interests. We can listen for the Lord's voice alone. We have more freedom to schedule and plan and not get swallowed up in details. We can be free from a whole bunch of concerns. We can develop relationships whenever and wherever the Lord leads. As we've already seen, this principle of freedom is so important, and marriage can so limit freedom, that *married* people are told to think and live "single" (see 1 Corinthians 7:29).

This doesn't mean that we should give up our essential freedom when we get married. Some marriages are actually in violation of Galatians 5:1, because one person has personal issues that drive him or her to be in control and impose a "yoke of slavery" on the other. These marriages end up being exhausting, not exhilarating. So what does this mean? We should be free if we are married. But we might be even more free if we're not.

Reason #2: Certainty. We have time to live well and make good decisions. We can learn who *we* are. We can learn who other people are. We can learn to live well in the spiritual, emotional, decision making, and financial areas of life. We can make sure that the timing in all of our relationships is appropriate, and that the pace of their development makes sense. We can gain perspective by knowing many people. Over time this will allow us to shed illusions about trust, loyalty, and perfection. We'll really know what people are like, so we can avoid the "you don't look like the person I thought I needed" problem. We can learn about our own strengths and weaknesses, how others can complement or magnify our weaknesses, and how others can zap or increase our strength.

Reason #3: Impact. We can impact a greater number of people. We can touch more lives since we have less "details of life" and time demands. In marriage, we must sometimes sacrifice breadth (affecting a lot of people and ministries) because of responsibility for greater depth (affecting a spouse and children). This impact includes loving many people. Singleness doesn't limit love. In fact, it may allow you to love more people more freely. You won't have to deal with the "he's mine, why is he talking to her" problem, or at least you'll be able to escape from the jealous friend. You will probably have more resources to invest in others, in part because it isn't true that two can live more cheaply than one. Expectations go up, and you might end up buying a lot of things that you couldn't imagine needing when you were single.

Reason #4: Performance. You can always go from being single to being married, but it's tough to go the other way. The debris from a bad marriage, a separation, or a divorce can live on forever. It will definitely slow you down. Being able to say "I got gypped" won't make you feel any better. Just the daily annoyances of life and the emotional drain of trying to make a relationship work can exhaust the soul. A single person has only one person to slow him down—himself. A married person has two.

Reason #5: Opportunity. We have the chance to become whole. We can take the time to let God love us and to love what He's created us to be. A lot of people talk about the love of God, but they don't really feel or believe it. They end up looking for it in another human being. We can learn the pleasure of taking personal responsibility. We can avoid the expectation that someone else should or will do it for us (and blaming her when she doesn't). We can make sure we are enjoying our lives, and avoid inflicting our misery on others in the hope that they will somehow make it better.

Reason #6: Maturity. We can have a maturity that can match the level of decision about relationships. Maturity seeks and recognizes maturity. We can bring a whole, developing, valuable being to the table (us) in any relationship, in *all* relationships. In part, we gain this maturity by going through many trials with a good attitude (see James 1:2–4)—no easy trick. We can get past the "danger zone," the time when relationships often fall apart and marriages can go through traumatic reevaluation—ages twenty-five to twenty-nine for women and thirty to thirty-four for men.[4]

Reason #7: Commandment. We are told not to seek a spouse. Scripture forbids it (see 1 Corinthians 7:27b). The scary part is that if we look, we may *find* one (because we are predisposed and open to less than the best). The purpose of the commandment is not to inflict a burden on us, but to keep us from inflicting one on ourselves. If you don't look, and *the one* isn't out there waiting for you, you won't end up settling for "the billionth."

How should I view and approach relationships with the opposite sex? Aloof? Cautious? Open? Involved?

It's easy to swing to extremes on this one.

We can go into the relationship thinking either, *This is the greatest thing ever* or *This is totally scary.*

Neither extreme is the right answer. The opposite sex isn't the answer to life's questions, and it isn't the source of all danger.

The real answer? When we approach relationships with the opposite sex, we should be aloof. And cautious. And open. And involved.

Aloof. You shouldn't pour yourself into any relationship too quickly. If you don't do your warm-ups, you will definitely tear a muscle—a soul muscle. Let the relationship evolve like a fine dinner out, a dining experience that has five courses and takes three hours. If there is real friendship there, time is on your side. If there isn't real friendship there, time is on your side.

Cautious. There are some really scary people out there. Some of them are attractive and funny and smart and charming, but they're still scary. Maybe those things make them even *more* scary.

There are wolves and lunatics and users and leeches. Proceed with caution.

Open. You never know who the gems are, so you've got to be open. You've got to be vulnerable. How many great friendships have never been born because one or both people were too scared to open up? You've got to lay yourself out there, and be willing to risk some relational wounds.

Involved. The only way to affect people is to be involved in their lives, to be involved with them on the project of living. At times, you've got to throw yourself recklessly into life, pour yourself out, and let your enthusiasm lead the way.

Approach your relationships with all four of these in mind. You'll be able to throw out the bad apples and make a great pie with the good ones.

What should I be getting out of my singleness?

The most important thing to get out of your singleness is joy.

"What has happened to all your joy?" (Galatians 4:15 NIV) Paul asked. We're supposed to rejoice in the Lord *always* (see Philippians 4:4). If your singleness isn't bringing you joy, you're missing something very important. Ask God to show you the way to joy, in the middle of your singleness. *Because* of your singleness.

Another of the most important things to get out of your singleness is a wide view of the world. This includes knowing, understanding, evaluating, and caring about a lot of people. It's a time to grow out of selfishness and self-centeredness and into a willingness to give back something to others and to life.

Selfishness doesn't disappear with marriage. In fact, if you see a person who is selfish with everyone but his romantic interest, you can be sure that he will be selfish with his partner after the glow wears off.

Singleness is a time to expand your citizenship. It starts with developing your citizenship in the kingdom of heaven (see Philippians 3:20). Then it moves on to becoming a citizen of the world. Everyone on this planet was made by God, and many of them are worth knowing. Now is the time to know them.

What role should family and church play in my life while I'm single?

Families through the centuries have ranged in their involvement to planning the lives of young people and selecting their spouses on the one hand, to "hands off" on the other.

Regardless of the "system," they almost always have an opinion about your life. "You should go on with your schooling," "that job's beneath you," "you should never leave that great job," "he's a terrible influence on you," etc. Sometimes this advice is valuable; sometimes it's nonsense. Smart people take the time to see which it is, and then follow the good advice.

From your perspective, you shouldn't need to have your family plan your life. And unless your family is really evil—I mean monsters, not just obnoxious—you shouldn't want them completely out of the picture. So they have a role. A *defined* role.

Families need to find a balance between support and skepticism. If parents and other family members lean too heavily either way, they can push a person into a premature or ugly marriage. People can end up either trying to live up to expectations or rebelling against opposition. Here are seven key points to keep in mind, so your family won't pressure you to date someone you may want to keep just as a friend. You don't want to be pushed into marrying someone you've just begun to date.

Point #1: First impressions count. It's important to know how to handle early meetings between friends you might date and your family. Some families need more cautious handling than others, but the general rule is to get everyone acquainted as soon as possible. This lets you access your family's wisdom (however small that is) and it lets your friend get a feel for your roots. Try to make the first meeting one that allows a little relaxed conversation, rather than rushing out the door.

Point #2: More communication is generally the right answer. There's a strategy to knowing when and how to have longer and more penetrating conversations with your parents and family about your singleness or potential dates. Don't wait for them to come to you. They will feel shut out, and you will feel like they're nagging or trying to control you. But let them know what the ground rules are: "Dad, I want to make this decision, but I'd like your input." You're taking the lead in establishing adult conversation with your family.

Point #3: Your family can't get good answers if they don't ask good questions. Give your family some effective and non-annoying questions to ask you about your life and relationships. Don't assume they know what to ask; they probably don't. Nobody gets training in this stuff, at least until now (with the training you're giving them). Here are a few: "Since we're from the same family and have the same background, can you tell me where I'm likely to make mistakes in friendships?" "Would you tell me what you think are the strongest and weakest traits of this friend I'm thinking of dating?" "How do you think I will be different in two years if I spend a lot of time with this person?" Go back through the chapters in this book for ideas. There are a lot of other questions you can ask to set the framework for dialogue with your family.

Point #4: You can give your family permission to disagree. You don't need them to like all of your friends as much as you do. Or at all. Let them have their own opinions. You never know; they might be right once in a while. Only a fool would want to hear only positive statements (like "you *sound* like you're happy and in love"), and you're no fool. You don't want to hear just what your itching ears want to hear (like "you should go with your feelings because you know him better than I do"), because you're smart enough to know that your ears will be itching a lot!

Because you're smart, you'll look closely for any warning flags in their comments. You should want all of your family's thoughts and feelings, especially their disagreements, so you can have a range of opinions to guide you into wisdom.

Point #5: You should ask your family to keep their own emotions and needs out of your relationships. It's easy for our parents and siblings and others to push us into relationships that *they* are sure will be perfect. You see it in the Bible in Jacob's love for Rachel. Laban deceived Jacob. After making him jump through seven years' worth of hoops, he slipped a *Leah* into the honeymoon in *Rachel's* clothing.[5]

The influence and interference of family can push you into a marriage that you weren't looking for and, if you're not careful, into a *bad* marriage. They can push you because of a whole range of lousy reasons: they want you out of the house; they think this is the best you can do; they like your friend and want her around; they are attracted to your friend and are in some weird way marrying her through you. Have a clear conversation. Have it from time to time to keep it fresh. It might be hard, but you'll be glad you did.

Point #6: You could tell your family what to do (and not to do) when they see doubts in either you or your friends. If the doubts come (the BIG doubts), family can be an asset or a liability. Ling and Adrian had dated seriously for almost two years. Right before they were engaged, they both ended up with doubts. Even though they liked each other and cared about each other, they just didn't feel that they were ready for marriage. Enter Ling's mother, who spent a lot of time with each of them alone to convince them that their doubts were "normal" and that they should go ahead. The result was a mediocre marriage.

Let your family know that you want them to be a sounding board for you when you have doubts—to listen and ask questions and give examples, but not to pressure you into a certain decision. You need to learn to make your own decisions. Even if your decisions are less than perfect, they'll still be yours.

Point #7: Your family needs guidelines on how to react to the disagreements and wounds in your relationships. It's very easy for your family to run to the rescue when they see you hurting or your relationships causing pain. Once again, your family can take over your problems and pain and relationship if you're not careful. Instead, you need them to be a sounding board. You need their advice, so you'll know how to handle the hurt, deal with the conflict, and know when to restore and when to walk away.

What about your friends' families? One of the most important roles of their families is to give you a visual heads-up. If you see that your friend has a horrible mother or father, don't assume that she didn't pick up any of that. In fact, she might have become just like that parent, only right now she's younger and cuter than that horrible parent. Her parents will provide a window into her soul.

If you get serious about a friend who comes from a terrible family, you're playing with fire. He may have broken the generational chains, but you should take even longer to commit and give yourself plenty of time to see the effects of his family on him. And even if he is different, you're still going to have to deal with his awful family. Someone once said, "If a child of God marries a child of the devil, that child of God is sure to have some trouble with his father-in-law."

And if you don't know enough about her family to know how they have affected her, you don't know enough to marry her.

What is the role of your church in your single life?

Your church should be there to help you learn how to celebrate your singleness. They should provide people to be sounding boards. They should create a safe place to discuss dangerous ideas, like when to avoid certain people and what a single person should do about sex.

If your church is really interested in supporting young people and preventing poor or bad marriages, it should make it harder to get *married*, not divorced. "American churches have become blessing machines and wedding factories that don't really help couples bond for life," said Michael J. McManus. Many youth and singles groups don't exist to maximize the joy of single life. They have become a place to provide opportunities for people to meet and marry.

And why should young people and singles and married people be "split up" into separate groups anyway? When twenty-something people are put into a separate group, "young marrieds," while their single peers carry on in a singles group, the church has created a wall of hurt and added insidious pressure to the singles to get married so they can "graduate."

And churches can talk about the benefits of time to help young people make good decisions. Many people spend more time picking a career and a house than they do a spouse.

What if I'm single with one or more children? Shouldn't I get married so my children can have two parents?

Perhaps you are a single parent and feel this "driver" from another angle—wanting to have a father or mother for your children if you are widowed, divorced, or have had a baby outside of marriage.

Marrying in order to provide a second parent for children often ends up creating more problems than it solves. These problems can range from differences in parenting approaches to unshared family goals and directions. At the worst, difficulties can include stepparent abuse of children, an ugly reality that statistics consistently show is *significantly* higher than with natural parents. To know that we have invited abuse into our homes is surely a heavy burden to bear.

Even though the Bible suggests that younger widows marry again (see 1 Timothy 5:14), it doesn't say they should *look* for a husband. If a person is single due to an earlier divorce, there are a number of issues that should be addressed even after we think through God's teaching about remarriage (see Romans 7:2–4; Mark 10:1–12; Luke 16:18). The mistakes that led to the failure of the earlier marriage may impact the success of the second. Statistics show that second marriages fail at a higher rate than first ones, and third marriages at a higher rate than second ones.

In any case, there are important questions to be asked and answered: Am I really ready to commit to another lifetime relationship? Am I marrying for the sake of the relationship itself, or just for the children? Will this person be able and willing to be a good parent to my children? Will he or she develop a reasonable and effective connection with them? Will my children accept this person as their parent?

Unless we can answer these with a strong yes, we would do better to claim the wonderful promise that God will be a "father to the fatherless" (Psalm 68:5 NIV). What does this mean? He will truly be a Father to our children—provide for them, care for them, love them, nurture them, discipline them, and encourage them. Everything that a human father or mother can do, God can do in great measure.

Many people insist that children need two parents. One good parent clearly beats two bad ones, but one good parent may also beat a good parent entangled with a bad one. Enjoy your singleness. Enjoy being a single mom (or dad). You don't need another person in order to do a good job of parenting. You just need God and His people to help you become a good parent—the best ever.

Conclusion

Singleness and marriage aren't enemies. They're two different ways to live. One isn't better than the other.

Discounting and trading in your singleness too soon or foolishly is a waste.

Valuing and celebrating your singleness—now *that's* wisdom.

Discussion Questions

On Your Own

- *Ask Yourself:* What are the things I value most about being single? What do I think I am missing by being single? What will getting married cost me?

- *Ask Your Parents:* What did you miss most about your singleness when you got married? What are the three most important things a person should do while he or she is still single?

- *Ask Your Youth Pastor or Pastor.* Would you talk about the single life with the same intensity and in the same quantity that you talk about the married life? Would you help me celebrate my singleness? Would you tell our group about mediocre and ugly marriages, not just good ones, so we will have some balance? What do you think is best about being single?

- *Ask a Single Friend:* What are at least five things that you treasure about your singleness? What is the best thing about being single? What is the hardest thing about being single? What do you think people gain by giving up their singleness to get married? What do you think they lose?

Sexuality throws no light upon love,
but only through love can we learn to understand sexuality.
Rosenstock-Huessy

dealing with sex
chapter 12

Let me say right off the bat that it's OK if this is the first place you turned in the book when you saw the title in the table of contents. Because this is an interesting topic. A *very* interesting topic.

If sex wasn't so interesting and exciting, it wouldn't be jammed so much into movies, television programs, books, and magazines. It wouldn't be advertised on the billboards and on the stage and at the beach or the pool. If sex wasn't so interesting to almost everyone, a lot of beautiful stars would be working at McDonald's.

Sex can take us to a different place, full of romance and drama and pleasure and thrills. It can tantalize, excite, and seduce. It offers the hope of being loved in a fantastically intimate way by some electrifying person.

When we come down to it, sex is one of the most exciting things on the planet. Many of those who have experienced its fullness—not just its physical exhilaration but its lifting of the spirit and filling of the soul—would agree that it *is* one of the most exciting things on the planet.

The demon in sex is lust. True sexuality leads to humanness, but lust leads to depersonalization. Lust captivates rather than emancipates, devours rather than nourishes.[1]
Richard J. Foster

But the first quote at the top of this chapter hits the target. If you're not smart, you can focus on sex and dabble with sex and throw yourself into sex, and never learn a thing about love. In fact, the more you do these things, the further from understanding or experiencing love you will get. It's like dynamite—useful and exciting, and likely to blow you up if you don't know what you're doing.

Sexuality is truly one of the great and wonderful creations of God. But it's like a secret code. You can see what's before your eyes, but you can only *really* see what's there through the use of a special light. It's a light that lets you *decode sex.* It's the light of love, and without it you'll never have a clue about sex—about good sex, great sex, out-of-this-world sex.

You'll just have sex. All by itself. *Boring.* You may not believe it right now, but you should.

Because there is real irony in sex. By holding sex in front of our eyes continuously, and by letting others push sex in front of our eyes continuously, we are prevented from ever really seeing it.

We'll only see the physical stuff. The mechanical stuff. And we really won't see anything because all by itself those things are illusion. They will never satisfy. They will lead to more sex, and then worse sex, and then ugly sex, and then finally, to sex that will destroy your soul.

You're smarter than that and better than that. You can use the light, and decode sex.

Leading with Sex

Here's an interesting thing about us as human beings, which is also a problem: Our spirits and minds and hearts and wills are invisible, and only our bodies are visible. And yet, our bodies are only a fraction of who we are.

It's like the iceberg that sank the *Titanic.* Only a small part of it was visible above the waterline. From a safe distance, I'm sure it was beautiful. But in the wrong place, it caused total destruction.

The captain and crew of the *Titanic* had no idea how much ice was floating near their ship. They probably couldn't even imagine it. A little ice floating on the surface wouldn't have sunk that huge ocean liner. But that surface ice was attached to a *mountain* of ice below the surface of the sea. That's how spirit and mind and heart and will are. They're all there, hidden below the waterline, hard to see even when you're right next to a person and holding hands.

And this is the problem when we lead with sex. When we put sex and sexual things in the front of our relationship, we're ignoring the rest of the iceberg. We're ignoring the mountain of personality and being that is below what we can see. And our ship is likely to get sunk.

But it is so easy to lead with sex. How we look, how attractive we are, how *sexy* we are can become a dominant thought, even if we don't know how to do it. We still want people to think that we're exciting, that we're desirable, that we're downright *erotic*. Even if we don't feel that way right now, the thought will probably come as we grow and face the onslaught of sexual things in the culture around us.

When we lead with sex, not only are we putting just a small part of who we are "out there"; we're also sending signals to others that *this is the total of who we are.* We are physical. We are sexual. What you see is what you get. Believe me, if that's what you offer, they'll try to get it.

You can lead with sex. If you do, you'll end up craving sex and—amazingly—hating it at the same time.

Leading with the Soul

Smart people lead with their souls, with their *being.*

They don't want to be cheapened, to be turned into somebody's trinket or toy.

They develop their minds, hearts, and wills so they can think, feel, and act with purpose and meaning. They do it because it makes them better people. And they do it because it draws better people to them.

Smart people develop their bodies, too, because their bodies are an expression of who God made them to be. But they keep this in perspective. They know that nothing is more ordinary than a person who is beautiful on the outside and a disaster inside. They want to be really attractive *all the way through.*

Leading with the soul says, "I want the best for my life. I know that sex is a gift to me. God gave it to me. He made me a man [or woman], he made other men [and women], he made me with passions and desires and hormones. But I want this gift to make me better, not worse. I want it to lift me up, not tear me down. I want it to be part of a very joyous life—not the destroyer of my joy."

Leading with the soul isn't selfish or self-centered. It's self-control, self-direction, self-care, and self-enhancement.

Protect your soul. You only have one. But lead with it. Let those who only want you to lead with sex lose interest in you. Let them evaporate. Let them play their sexual games with one another. Let them play their sexual games with idiots—but not with you, because you're no idiot.

Leading with Love

Smart people also lead with love.

They realize that their lives are meant to be something majestic, "a living sacrifice" (Romans 12:1). They know that God is love (see 1 John 4:8). They know that the greatest commandment is to love God, and the second is to love other people with the same care and attention that they love themselves (see Matthew 22:37–39).

Leading with love is like the relational equivalent to the Hippocratic Oath that doctors used to take ("Do thy patient no harm"). "Love does no wrong to a neighbor. Love, therefore, is the fulfillment of the law" (Romans 13:10). Smart people know that real love nourishes, even in the midst of disagreements and arguments.

They know that love which does harm is a phony love. In fact, it's no love at all.

Smart people know that if they lead with love, they can be sure that they'll use their bodies as the right kind of sacrifice, as the right kind of *instrument.* "Do not offer any parts of it to sin as weapons for unrighteousness. But as those who are alive from the dead, offer yourselves to God, and all the parts of yourselves to God as weapons for righteousness" (Romans 6:13).

Smart people see that they can offer their bodies, including their sexuality, as a tool of goodness. They work hard to find out how to do so.

People are always talking about "God's will" and obeying God. Here's what Jesus said: "This is what I command you: that you love one another" (John 15:17). He's telling us that obedience starts with love.

In every relationship you have for the rest of your life, you can do no better than to lead with love.

Sex the Wrong Way

There are a number of ways to take a really exquisite thing like sex and mess it up big-time. Here are a few:

Sex That Is Too Sterile

God told us to "be fruitful and increase in number" (Genesis 1:28 NIV), but He didn't tell us that this is the *only* or *most important* thing we could do.

Through the centuries, the church has tended to teach that the main purpose of sex is to have children. This is a pretty sterile attitude, and one that reduces the beauty and power of sex down to human breeding. If you don't see how fulfilling sex surrounded by love can be, but still see that it's necessary for the human race to continue, you end up with a theology of human breeding.

God doesn't tell us that children are the only or the major reason to have sex. All you have to do is read the Song of Solomon in the Bible to see that God has a *whole* lot more in mind for sex than that.

And although God told us to increase in number, He didn't give us the number. God didn't put us here just to breed more people. Besides, if you have a lot of children at the expense of developing yourself, you will end up breeding a lot of *ignorant* people. How can your children know anything if you're their teacher and *you* don't know anything?

This is one of the reasons that Bernard Lewis, an expert on Islam and the Middle East, gives for the decline of fundamentalist Islamic cultures. He says Islam has moved from the position of being the leading culture in the world five hundred years ago to one of the most backward today. One of the reasons is that they don't expect or allow women to be educated and ambitious, but they *do* expect them to train and become the prime caretakers of the next generation of young men.[2]

Any parent can raise children to be ignorant and incompetent, *if the parent is.*

Don't let anyone reduce the awesome wonder of sex into a means of having more people who don't know what sex is for.[3]

Sex That Is Too Soon

What about premarital sex?

Even if you're serious about each other, it's not a good idea because it moves you from leading with soul and leading with love into leading with sex. And it's the wrong thing to do because it's against God's plan. It will leave you both feeling smaller than you did before. It will leave you with guilt and shame and a sense that something good has been lost. It's a bad idea.

One of the legends of our culture (and many others) is the idea of the *shotgun wedding.* This comes from an old concept that forcing a marriage where there has been premarital sex (and particularly if a pregnancy has resulted) somehow makes the sin right.

But how can the sin itself be a basis for a godly and decent marriage? How can the breaking of these boundaries and the absence of self-control point the way toward a marriage that will last and go deep with God? These conditions are just as likely—perhaps more likely—to indicate a basic flaw in the relationship and in the individual spiritual lives. The resulting problems will either have to be sorted out later on, or they will cause the death of the marriage.

Heather and Steve had gone together for over two years. Everyone thought they were "it." After Heather got pregnant, her mother, two sisters, and pastors counseled her to marry Steve. Heather had reservations about Steve and even more about marriage. She thought about raising her child by herself, but after several weeks of pressure she finally yielded. She and Steve got married.

But no one had dealt with the underlying problems in the relationship or in the hearts of the two people involved. The result in this case was a grievous marriage to an empty man, who abused Heather and her daughter verbally, emotionally, and sexually.

Premarital sex is not only a poor reason to marry. It can also be devastating to any marriage that comes out of it. William Congreve said, "Thus grief still treads upon the heels of pleasure, marry'd in haste, we may repent at leisure." In fact, those who are sexually active before marriage have a significantly higher chance of someday being separated or divorced from their spouses.[4]

Sex That Is Too Quick

Some people see sex as an event rather than as a process. They will skip the kissing and hugging and holding to get to the climax, because the rest is process and it just isn't that important.

One of King David's sons, Amnon, saw it this way with a beautiful woman named Tamar. He wanted to have sex with her, but he "became frustrated to the point of illness . . . for she was a virgin, and it seemed impossible for him to do anything to her" (2 Samuel 13:2 NIV). He and a friend developed a plan for him to do something to her, and he did. But then we're told an interesting thing.

After he had raped her, he "hated her with intense hatred. In fact, he hated her more than he had loved her."[5]

This is the way it goes with sex when it is viewed as some solitary event, rather than as part of a deep love and an ongoing commitment. After the sex is over, what the person thought was love is over, too.

People who aren't smart want sex too quick for a number of reasons:

- They don't understand how to be a real friend. They undervalue the soul side of the other person and the real intimacy that is possible, both to have and to offer the other.
- They think of sex as a current statement of closeness. This is the "if you loved me, you'd . . ." problem. Some people just can't feel close to another person unless there is sex involved. It's a statement of shallowness, not depth.
- They confuse sex with intimacy. They don't understand that sex is a seal of intimacy, but it isn't the intimacy itself. Real intimacy is an eye-to-eye, mind-to-mind, heart-to-heart, soul-to-soul connection that is so vivid you almost can't believe it's yours. False intimacy is clashing bodies and smashing souls.

Sex That Is Too Ugly

Every good thing in life has a shadow.

The enjoyment of good food can turn into gluttony. Appreciating the way God made you can change into self-centeredness. Righteous indignation can morph into uncontrolled rage. Zeal for God can become religious lunacy. Reverence for God's law can transform into fierce judgmentalism.

And the enjoyment of things sexual—that she's a girl, that he's a boy, that she's so beautiful, that he's so handsome—can turn into lust. Lust is the shadow of sex.

"Many people will enter a marriage relationship based upon lust rather than love," says Richard Foster, "simply because the two often look so much alike . . . . Lust produces bad sex, because it denies relationship."[6]

But *at the core,* sex and lust are *not* very much alike. When lust finally takes off its mask, we can see how horrible it is. For example, in a recent survey of more than four thousand high school girls, "one in five reported date-related physical or sexual violence. The statistics may even be worse among college students."[7]

This is not coincidental. Many people believe that sexual assaults are really a form of rage, violence, and control. Lust, when it is fully grown up, is about rage, violence, and control. It's like a terrorist trying to hijack your body and crash it into a wall.[8]

Some people don't think one person is enough to satisfy sexual desires. But, said Balzac, "It is as absurd to say that a man can't love one woman all the time as it is to say that a violinist needs several violins to play the same piece of music." One person, if he or she is the right person, is enough.

If you have a serious problem with lust—you can't seem to stop the flood of lustful thoughts about the people in your life, you think and dream about sexual things constantly—you are not ready for marriage. You're not ready even for close relationships. You've got some homework to do, and it's critical for you to do that homework if you want to have a great life.

If you're not careful, lust can end up dominating your whole life—every minute, every hour, every day, forever. Lust is not talked about like drugs or alcohol, but it is every bit as addictive. You'll end up needing a "fix." It will reorient your mind to see everything—every person, every movie, every book—through the eyes of lust. You will end up craving sex, and it will get you to do things that you couldn't even imagine doing. It may even bring physical and chemical changes in your body which will push you further down that miserable road. If you have this type of problem, ask for God's help and consider asking a wise, trustworthy mentor to help.

And if you don't have a serious problem with lust, you should take lots of precautions to make sure you don't spend time with people who do. They will rub off on you. You'll take down doors and walls that will open you up to thinking things that you don't want to think. Believe me, *you don't want to think these things.*

And as we said in chapter 7, you don't want to marry a person who has a serious problem with lust. You won't be the cure. You'll be a short-term fix that will never satisfy what he or she is craving. You should pray for this person—from a distance. "Better to sit up all night," said Jeremy Taylor, "than to go to bed with a dragon."

Now let's take a moment to clear up something on this issue of lust: Temptations aren't sins. Tempting *thoughts* aren't sins. They are thoughts. People who say you're sinning if you have an "impure thought" are holding up a wrong standard.[9]

Temptations come from outside our spirits. They come from the Enemy or the corrupt world system or our own sinful natures. They are alien. And they aren't sinful unless we give them a home—unless we dwell on them, absorb them, make them our own, give into them.

Sex that is ugly is *really* ugly.

But sex that is beautiful is—beautiful.

Last Thoughts

The reality is that all of us have to come to terms with sex.

Here's the truth: You can be married and immoral. Just like you can be single and moral. Morality isn't a function of your relationships with people. It's a function of your relationship with *God*.

The clash of bodies has no meaning apart from a whole-being relationship. Pleasure has no ultimate meaning apart from a whole-being relationship. If that relationship doesn't exist, sex has a harmful relationship with your soul: The more you do it, the less you are. You'll feel empty and drained of life. What seemed like a worthy goal or conquest will end up a big fat zero.

Loving another human being is a whole-being activity. You can love and be loved *wholly* and *holy*. And sex can be a glorious part of it. Sex is one of the greatest gifts ever given by God to human

194

beings, and it's worth waiting to share it with *the one,* rather than wasting it on empty relationships. So be grateful.

But don't be greedy.

Discussion Questions

On Your Own

- *Ask Yourself:* What role do I think sex plays in a male-female relationship? What are my expectations about sex? What do I fear about sex? What limits will I obey to ensure that I will not dishonor God or take advantage of any person?

- *Ask Your Parents:* Can you tell me what you've learned about what makes sex great and what makes sex ugly?

- *Ask Your Youth Pastor or Pastor:* Would you create a safe place for us to talk about sexual issues openly and honestly? Would you teach us how to use ourselves as instruments of righteousness, not wickedness?

Together

- *Ask Each Other:* How important is sex to you? Why? How can we keep ourselves as instruments of righteousness?

No one has ever loved anyone the way everyone wants to be loved.
Mignon McLaughlin

a few last thoughts

conclusion

Your life can be the most astonishing thing on this planet.

You can live a smart, wise, interesting, and exciting life. You can live like almost no one has ever lived. You can live a life worthy of what God put into you, a life worthy of being lived. You can *have* the real deal.

And you can love others in a smart, wise, interesting, and exciting way. You can do that like almost no one has ever done. You can love people in a worthy way, a love worthy of what God put into them, a love worthy of being shared. You can *offer* the real deal.

At the end of your life, you'll know fully what you may already see: The only great life is one lived with character and passion.

If you live your life with character—with wholeness and integrity and dignity and class—you will be a person worth knowing. You will stand out like a rainbow at the end of a fierce storm. And, if marriage is for you, you will *be* a person worth marrying.

If you live your life with passion—with commitment and energy and compassion—you will find many people worth knowing. You will leave a beautiful trail of nourished souls behind you. And if it's for one of them (as well as you), you will *find* a person worth marrying.

If you're out there for each other—two people becoming people worth knowing and marrying—you will know it. You will know it, because you will take the time to make sure you're marrying for the right reasons. You will know it, because you will make sure of some important things before you marry. And you will know it, because you've taken the time to learn the secrets of knowing you've found *the one.*

The quote at the beginning of this chapter said, "No one has ever loved anyone the way everyone wants to be loved."

If you do life right, really right, you can be the one to love that way.

And to be loved—the way you want to be loved.

notes

chapter 1

1. This doesn't mean that these trials are bad or useless; on the contrary, they lead to perseverance and maturity. But the "teacher" is discipline, and a big chunk of pain.

chapter 2

1. See 1 Thessalonians 2:19–20 for one of the most remarkable truths of human relationship.

2. Philippians 2:3b NIV. You might want to look up the first half of this verse—it's very serious and pretty astonishing.

3. I suggest you take plenty of personality, aptitude, and other sorts of evaluation tools. Get lots of advice. Make sure you understand yourself. Most of us are too young to make career decisions when we have to make them, but we can at least make them as intelligently as possible. And if we get into something and there is no fire, we should drop it in a New York minute.

4. See James 1:2, where it says we're supposed to choose to make even trials a joy. And see also Hebrews 13:17, which talks about how we can make the work of leaders either a burden or a joy.

5. Paul's advice to Timothy in 1 Timothy 4:15 NIV.

6. You have to think hard to make sure you've picked something great and not phony. You have to develop a serious baloney detector. For instance, every generation of Christians gets excited about the end of the world. This is not a great cause. Instead of spending time on making the world a better place, bazillions of

Christians spend their time reading and talking about "the end." The problem is, nobody really knows what that will be like or when that will be. It's OK to read *Left Behind,* but only if you realize that, nice as they might be, Tim LaHaye and Jerry Jenkins don't know any more about the *timing* of the Second Coming than Bill Clinton or Madonna.

7.   Matthew 18:15 says if someone offends you, you're supposed to go to them. Matthew 5:23–24 says that if you offend someone else, you're supposed to go to them. Whoever started it, you're supposed to go first. If two people were both practicing these verses, they would *meet in the middle.* Can you do these things?

8.   1 Corinthians 9:22b NIV. Note that the reason Paul adapted was to see people *saved,* not to become more popular.

chapter 3

1.   See Proverbs 27:17. What happens when iron sharpens iron?

2.   This is based on the seven pillars of wisdom in James 3:17. Check it out compared with Proverbs 9:1—is James telling us clearly what those seven pillars described in Proverbs are?

chapter 4

1.   "Surf Here Often? Online Matchmaking Is Changing the Christian Dating Game," in *Christianity Today,* June 11, 2001.

2.   The great advice of superinvestor Warren Buffet, the "Sage of Omaha."

chapter 5

1.   "First Marriage Dissolution, Divorce, and Remarriage: United States," Centers for Disease Control, Number 323, May 31, 2001.

2.   "The Nature and Predictors of the Trajectory of Change in Marital Quality for Husbands and Wives over the First 10 Years of

Marriage: Predicting the Seven-Year Itch," in *Journal of Developmental Psychology,* September 1999.

3. Quoted in "Positive Illusions," *Time,* 27 September 1999, p. 112.

4. "One in Four British Couples Regret Marriage, Poll Says," Reuters Limited, December 18, 2001.

5. From "Can Generation Xers—many of whom are the children of divorce—make their own marriages last?" *Newsweek,* July 15, 1998, reported on AOL.

6. "If at First You Don't Succeed," *Time,* February 4, 2002, p.14.

7. Ibid.

8. "Courtship: 'More sexual, less emotional,' than years ago," *U.S. News & World Report,* 1984.

9. Did you know that a saline abortion actually burns the baby to death?

chapter 6

1. Les Parrott and Leslie Parrott, "Growing a Healthy Marriage" in *Christian Counseling Today,* Spring 1996, p. 18.

2. Note that God tells them that asking for a king to watch over them was "an evil thing" (v. 17). Asking for a husband or wife to make your decisions for you is no less evil, but if you ask you will likely receive it. And then you'll regret it, like the Israelites did.

3. See Matthew 5:33–37, where we're told to keep our language plain and unadorned.

chapter 7

1. See 2 Timothy 3:13, which tells us that this stuff always gets worse.

2. Proverbs 23:6–8 is a great summary of this problem. If you spend time with these people, you will end up feeling like you have to vomit.

3.   See Proverbs 21:9 and 25:24. Although it uses a wife as the example, you can rest assured that it works both ways.

4.   The examples Jesus used are related to giving, praying, and fasting. This must be an important issue for Him to cover it three different ways.

5.   Jesus said that people who judged others would be judged themselves, and according to the same standard. See Matthew 7:2.

chapter 8

1.   1 Samuel 20:17 NIV. Another translation says, "Jonathan made David reaffirm his vow of friendship again, for Jonathan loved David as much as he loved himself."

2.   There are many biblical passages that address this issue in very clear terms: Leviticus 18:22 and 20:13; Romans 1:21–27; 1 Corinthians 6:9; and 1 Timothy 1:10. It would be good for you to read them for yourself. However, it is just as clear that homosexuality is not some "unforgivable sin." The only unforgivable sin is to *blaspheme the Holy Spirit* (see Mark 3:28–29). The way you do that is to say that the Holy Spirit is lying when He tells you that Jesus is the Savior, which means that you don't believe He is the Savior and you choose hell instead. Also, the temptation to think homosexual thoughts or to commit homosexual practices is not a sin—no temptation is a sin. It's only the doing it that is sin. For an incredibly thoughtful and sensitive discussion of homosexuality and the Christian, see Richard Foster's book *The Challenge of the Disciplined Life* (New York: HarperSanFrancisco, 1985), pp. 106–112.

chapter 9

1.   Dr. Dan B. Allender, *Bold Love* (Colorado Springs: NavPress, 1992), 297.

chapter 10

1. See Genesis 29:17–20. Note the reason why the years seemed like a few days to Jacob. If days seem like years, you're probably pushing.

2. "At 20, a soul mate is a cool concept." *USA Today,* June 13, 2001.

chapter 11

1. "Solitary Confinement," *Christianity Today,* June 11, 2001, p. 36.

2. Too much of the church has also left verse 21 out of the exposition of the passage, even though the whole tone of this section is that there is something *mutual* about submission and marriage.

3. See 1 Corinthians 9:24–27. No spouse, no matter how terrific, can win your prize for you.

4. According to the National Center for Health Statistics.

5. The whole story is in Genesis chapter 29.

chapter 12

1. Richard J. Foster, *The Challenge of the Disciplined Life* (New York: HarperSanFrancisco, 1985), p. 13. I recommend this book to you highly. A third of the book is devoted to sex, singleness, and marriage, and is well worth your time.

2. If you want a very interesting read, get his book *What Went Wrong?* (New York: Oxford University Press, 2002). It's a short book, packed with interesting stuff.

3. A lot of Christians have condemned the philosophy, espoused by Hegel and others, that says a thing is good only if it's useful (it's called *utilitarianism*). But that's what too many Christians have said about sex—it's only good if it's "useful."

4. Joan R. Kahn and Kathryn A. London, "Premarital Sex and the Risk of Divorce," *Journal of Marriage and the Family* 54 (Nov. 1991), 845–55.

5. The whole ugly story is told in 2 Samuel 13.

6. Foster, ibid., pp. 14 and 99.

7. "Alarming data on dating violence," in *Bottom Line Personal*, March 15, 2002, p. 15.

8. See Romans 6:4.

9. For example, the "Colorado Statement on Biblical Sexual Morality" says, "God's standard is purity in every thought about sex . . . Sexual purity is violated even in thoughts that never lead to outward acts." This turns every tempting thought into a sin, and spreads loads of unnecessary guilt around in a world full of tempting thoughts. Martin Luther said, "I can't keep the birds from flying around my head, but I can keep them from making a nest in my hair." Letting thoughts "make the nest" in our actions is the sin.

Also Available

The TruthQuest™ Inductive Student Bible (NLT)
    Black bonded leather with slide tab 1-55819-843-1
    Blue bonded leather with slide tab 1-55819-849-0
    Paperback with Expedition Bible Cover 1-55819-928-4
    Hardcover 1-55819-855-5
    Paperback 1-55819-848-2
    Expedition Bible Cover only 1-55819-929-2

The TruthQuest™ Share Jesus without Fear New Testament
(HCSB) 1-58640-013-4

The TruthQuest™ Prayer Journal 0-8054-3777-0

The TruthQuest™ Devotional Journal 0-8054-3800-9

TruthQuest™ Books

Survival Guide: The Quest Begins!
by Steve Keels with Dan Vorm
0-8054-2485-7

Coming May 1, 2004
Survival Guide Spanish Edition
En Busca de la Verdad—
Plan de Accion
0-8054-3045-8

You Are Not Your Own:
Living Loud for God
by Jason Perry of Plus One
with Steve Keels
0-8054-2591-8

Living Loud: Defending Your Faith
by Norman Geisler & Joseph Holden
0-8054-2482-2

Getting Deep: Understand What
You Believe about God and Why
by Gregg R. Allison
0-8054-2554-3

Vision Moments: Creating Lasting
Truths in the Lives of Your Students
by Bo Boshers & Keith Cote
0-8054-2725-2

Something from Nothing:
Understand What You Believe
about Creation and Why
by Kurt Wise & Sheila Richardson
0-8054-2779-1

Commentaries

Coming July 15, 2004
Getting Deep in the Book of . . .
    Luke: Up Close with Jesus
    0-8054-2852-6
    James: Christian to the Core
    0-8054-2853-4
Coming September 15, 2004
    Romans: A Life and Death
    Experience
    0-8054-2857-7
    Revelation: Never Say Die
    0-8054-2854-2
by Steve Keels
& Lawrence Kimbrough

Available at Your Local Book Retailer

BROADMAN
& HOLMAN
PUBLISHERS
www.broadmanholman.com/truthquest

Praise for A Perfect Persecution
A Novel about the Future
by James R. Lucas

"Wow! This book will absolutely change your life . . . . It is well written, suspenseful, and gripping. It will make your heart ache to stop what has already begun in our great country."
Kimberly Pharris, Bowling Green, Kentucky

"A perfect plot. This is one of the best Christian fiction books ever! . . . The plot accelerates to pure action and suspense . . . . The story pits strong female protagonist Leslie Adams (a.k.a. Phoenix) against a villain who starts out sinister enough and becomes more and more chillingly evil as the plot, with all its twists and surprises, progresses. The climax was awesome."
Agent Sonica, reviewer, Amazon.com

"Set in the not-too-distant future, *A Perfect Persecution* will keep the reader on the edge of his chair."
Barbara Bryden, *Christian Library Journal*

"The futuristic novel . . . provides lots of food for thought. . . . The main character finds that one person can make a difference in society. . . . The characters are well developed; the plot is action packed and suspenseful. . . . Recommended."
Church Libraries Magazine

"Great book. I just finished this book, and it was absolutely wonderful!"
A reader from Des Moines, Iowa

"An amazing book with a powerful message. . . . This book brought to life for me many different subjects that have been brought up in the classroom this year. . . . This novel will alter the way you look at life and display how valuable and precious life is from its very start."
A reader from Dallas, Texas

"*A Perfect Persecution* is an unsettling and challenging view of the future . . . an intense and absorbing read."
The Baptist New Mexican

"Every so often a book comes along that radically alters what people think about the world. For example, *Uncle Tom's Cabin* made slavery unthinkable. And *1984* made totalitarianism intolerable. [*A Perfect Persecution*] is such a book."
Jan Dennis, Literary Agent and Former Editor